# Instructor's Manual

to accompany

Goshgarian/Krueger/Minc

# Dialogues: An Argument Rhetoric and Reader

*Third Edition*

Gary Goshgarian
*Northeastern University*

Kathleen Krueger

Janet Barnett Minc
*University of Akron – Wayne College*

*Prepared by*
Kathryn Goodfellow

# LONGMAN

An Imprint of Addison Wesley Longman, Inc.

New York • Reading, Massachusetts • Menlo Park, California • Harlow, England
Don Mills, Ontario • Sydney • Mexico City • Madrid • Amsterdam

*Instructor's Manual t/a Dialogues: An Argument Rhetoric and Reader, 3e*

ISBN: 0-321-06487-9

12345678910-CRS-02010099

# CONTENTS

# PREFACE

*Dialogues: An Argument Rhetoric and Reader, Third Edition,* encourages students to explore multiple perspectives on a particular issue before forming their own opinions and writing their own arguments. In Part One of the text, the chapters that introduce this approach are Chapters 1 and 2, although its practice informs the entire book. In Chapter 1, the process of "debate, dialogue, and deliberation" is presented as a process for evaluating and building arguments through comparing and synthesizing diverse viewpoints. Chapter 2 aids in this process by showing students how to read arguments critically, including how to analyze, evaluate, and argue with a reading. The organization of Part Two into sub-topics focused by specific questions also assumes that students will investigate multiple perspectives on each issue. Many of the questions in Part 2, especially the Writing Assignments at the end of each sub-topic, are designed to require synthesis of various points of view or analysis of conflicting information to spark students' recognition of the wide range of opinion on any topic worth arguing.

This *Instructor's Manual* provides two helpful tools for instructors planning their courses. First is a sample syllabus that outlines one possible course organization. The majority of the *Instructor's Manual* is the answers to all the questions in the book. We hope that these two basic planning tools will be helpful to you as you consider how best to organize your course and your assignments.

Numerous other ancillaries provide both printed and on-line support for *Dialogues, Third Edition.* The book's website, *Dialogues on the Web* (http://www.awlonline.com/goshgarian) includes additional activities and links to related sources; the Longman English Pages (http://www.longman.awl.com/englishpages) provide updated resources for reading, writing, and research practice. Please contact your local representative for further information about *Daedalus Online,* and the print ancillaries *Researching Online, The Longman Guide to Columbia Online*

*Style, The Essential Research Guide,* and our special offer of the *Penguin Program.*

# SAMPLE SYLLABUS
# FOR A SEMESTER-LENGTH COURSE

## WEEK 1

### Class 1
Course introduction
Journal Assignment: Find an article in a current newspaper or periodical (up to 6 months old) about a controversial issue which interests you. Use your journal to explore your understanding of the issue and your position on it. Bring in a copy of the article to accompany your journal entry.
Reading Assignment: Chapter 1

### Class 2
Discussion of Chapter 1 reading
Peer group work
Journal Assignment: Read in Chapter 12 Cannon, "Honey, I Warped the Kids," Scheer, "Violence Is Us," and Klavan, "In Praise of Gore." Analyze each writer's claim and the arguments used to support it. Which do you find most effective and which do you find unconvincing?
Reading Assignment: Chapter 2

## WEEK 2

### Class 1
Discussion and peer group work
Journal Assignment: Find an article in a current newspaper or periodical (up to 6 months old) about a controversial issue which interests you. Summarize the article, and then use the questions in "Analyze and Evaluate the Reading" (Chapter 2) to analyze and evaluate it.

### Class 2
Paired discussion: Introduce your issue to your partner by summarizing the issue, stating your own position on it, and discussing how the article

writer's position is similar to and different from your own. (Take no more than 10 minutes). Your partner should then do the same.
Class discussion
Reading Assignment: Chapter 4. Read carefully Koop, "Don't Forget the Smokers," Jacoby, "What the Antismoking Zealots Really Crave," and Samuelson, "Media Have Fallen for Misguided Antismoking Campaign." Be prepared to discuss the Questions for Analysis and Discussion.

## WEEK 3

Class 1
Discussion of readings, argumentative structure
Writing Assignment: Your first paper will present your position on a currently controversial issue of your choice. To begin, decide on the issue you will argue and your position. Focus on making your position clear and developing convincing key points to support it. Consider other possible perspectives, and possible objections to your point of view. Make two copies of your draft and bring to class.

Class 2
Peer group work on Draft #1
Student/teacher conferences
Reading: Chapter 5
Writing Assignment: Work on the second draft of your paper. Focus on evidence and examples that will make your view persuasive. Make two copies and bring to class.

## WEEK 4

Class 1
Peer group work on Draft #2
Student/teacher conferences
Writing workshop
Writing Assignment: Complete final draft of your position paper.

Class 2

Paper #1 due. Include all drafts and all peer group work in your paper folder.

Discussion of evidence

Journal Assignment: In Chapter 16, read Sylvester, "Teenage Pregnancy: A Preventable Calamity," Battin, "A Better Way of Approaching Teen Pregnancy," and Wilson, "'Charter Families: Hope for the Children of Illegitimacy?" Evaluate the solutions each writer offers for the problem of teen pregnancy. For each essay, what do you find most persuasive and least persuasive? What strategies did each writer use?

Reading Assignment: Chapter 6

WEEK 5

Class 1

Discussion and peer group work

Journal Assignment: Read in Chapter 16 Luker, "Constructing an Epidemic." Respond to Questions 1, 2, and 3 in the For Analysis and Discussion questions following the reading.

Class 2

Peer group work on debate and dialogue among Sylvester, Battin, Wilson, and Luker

Journal Assignment: Describe how you view the problem of teen pregnancy. Then discuss solutions you might propose to the problem as you have described it.

Research Assignment: Find and read two current articles (within the last 2-3 years) on a social issue that relates to teen pregnancy, as discussed in any of the articles we have read (for example, poverty). The articles may propose, support, or simply inform the reader about a solution to this social problem.

Bring the articles to class.

WEEK 6

Class 1
Discussion of articles and journals
Peer group work on dialogue and deliberation
Journal Assignment: Read in Chapter 9 Pipher, "Saplings in the Storm,"
and Pollack, "How U.S. Schools Are Stifling Male Students." If the two
writers were to engage in debate, dialogue, and deliberation, what would
they say to each other?

Class 2
Discussion of readings and journals
Journal Assignment: Read in Chapter 9 Gray, "Mr. Fix-It and the Home-
Improvement Committee," and Tannen, "I'm Sorry, I Won't Apologize."
What is your position on the difference in communication styles between
men and women (when talking to each other)? List the key points and
examples you would use to support your position.

WEEK 7

Class 1
Peer group work
Class discussion
Journal Assignment: Read in Chapter 10 Garvin, "Loco, Completamente
Loco," Rodriguez, "Bilingualism: Outdated and Unrealistic," Rovira,
"Let's Not Say Adios to Bilingual Education," and Yzaguierre, "What's
Wrong with Bilingual Education?" Explore how the various arguments
each writer makes are similar to and different from one another's. Which
arguments do you find most and least persuasive?

Class 2
Discussion of readings and journals
Journal Assignment: Refer to Question 2 in the Writing Assignments:
Bilingual Education. Visit the website and read the fact sheet and at least
two linked articles. Explore your own position on bilingual education,

supporting your viewpoint with information from at least two or three of the sources you have read on this topic.

WEEK 8

Class 1
Discussion of journals
Discussion of summary
Journal Assignment: Read in Chapter 13 Lewis, "Naïve Court Didn't Go Far Enough with Drug Testing," Natriello, "Testing for Drugs, Witches, and Leftover Milk," Rocah, "Just Say No to Random Drug Testing," and Will, "High Court Takes on School Athletes and Drug Testing." Select any two of these four articles and write a one-paragraph summary of each.

Class 2
Discussion of paraphrasing
Journal Assignment: Respond to Question 3 in the Writing Assignments: Students and Drug Testing by writing the first draft of a letter. Focus on the approach you will take to avoid the most conflict.

WEEK 9

Class 1
Discussion of journals
Discussion of quotation
Writing Assignment: Paper #2 will be a proposal argument on a social issue. You will be required to use and refer specifically to ideas from at least two sources in your paper to support, challenge, or inform; one of these may come from the essays in the text, but at least one must be from an article you find on your own. Include copies of sources you find with your final draft. To begin, decide on a specific problem or concern that you want to explore. (The more specific the problem, the easier it will be for you to create a credible solution.) In your journal, explain the problem or concern, your tentative solution, and how the solution will solve the problem.

Class 2
Peer group brainstorming for papers
Student/teacher conferences
Writing Assignment: Work on the first draft of your paper. Focus on explaining the problem clearly so that your reader will understand it and its importance. Include any personal experiences or examples to demonstrate the effect of the problem on the reader. Your solution needs to address those features of your problem. Make two copies and bring to class.

WEEK 10

Class 1
Peer group work on draft #1
Student/teacher conferences
Writing Assignment: Work on the second draft of your paper. In this draft, consider ways you can use ideas from your sources to strengthen your points or provide differing perspectives and opposing arguments. Make two copies and bring to class.

Class 2
Peer group work on draft #2
Student/teacher conferences
Writing Assignment: Complete your final draft for paper #2.

WEEK 11

Class 1
Paper #2 due. Include all drafts, peer group work, and copies of any outside sources in your paper folder. Highlight the parts of your sources that you summarized, paraphrased, or quoted from in your paper.
Discussion of evaluating sources
Journal Assignment: Read in Chapter 11 Cleaver, "The Internet: A Clear and Present Danger?," Wilkins, "Protecting Our Children from Internet Smut," and Bennett, "What Part of 'No Law' Don't You Understand?" In

your journal, identify the writers' arguments and discuss which arguments you find most persuasive and least persuasive in each article.

Class 2
Discussion of readings and journals
Journal Assignment: Locate two current articles (no more than 1 year old) from print and/or on-line sources on a topic involving freedom of expression. Evaluate each article in your journal, paying attention to the writer's purpose and audience, evidence, logic, and reliability of sources. Which article do you find most reliable? Why?

WEEK 12

Class 1
Discussion of articles and evaluations
Peer group work: Decide on a controversial issue you wish to explore and a strategy for finding articles and information to share with the rest of the class. In order to provide balance, you will need to locate sources which reflect a variety of arguments and viewpoints.
Assignment: Find sources for information about the issue your group has chosen to explore. Bring copies of your sources (articles, statistics, books, etc.) to class to share them with your group.

Class 2
Peer group work: Share articles and information with your group and prepare to discuss and explain your sources with the class. Figure out how to acquaint the class with the arguments on the various sides of the issue.
Assignment: Group decides assignment for each member to prepare for presentation.

WEEK 13

Class 1
Group presentations
Reading Assignment: Chapter 8

Journal Assignment: For one of the topics we've been exploring since the last paper, identify an issue you find interesting. In the library or on the Internet, find and evaluate two additional sources of information on the issue. Using summary, paraphrase, and/or quotation, take notes on the key arguments and details in each article.

Class 2
Discussion of integrating source material and attribution
Writing Assignment: Paper #3 will be an argumentative essay (position or proposal) on a controversial issue of your choice. It should use a minimum of three **outside** sources to provide examples, support, and challenges to your arguments. You may also use essays from the text **in addition to** these three if you wish. To begin work on your paper, decide on a specific controversial issue, and in your journal discuss the issue, your position, and the arguments you might use to support it.

WEEK 14

Class 1
Peer group work: Present your initial ideas to your group to get feedback and additional ideas for your paper.
Student/teacher conferences about paper topics
Assignment: Find the sources you will use in your paper. Summarize at least three of your sources. Begin the first draft of your paper.

Class 2
Source summaries due (attach copies of articles)
Discussion of documentation and the Works Cited list
Writing Assignment: Work on the first draft of your paper. Bring copies to class for peer group work.

WEEK 15

Class 1
Peer group work on draft #1

Student/teacher conferences
Writing Assignment: Work on the second draft of your paper.

Class 2
Peer group work on draft #2
Student/teacher conferences
Writing Assignment: Complete paper #3.

WEEK 16

Class 1
Paper #3 due. Include all drafts, peer group work, and copies of sources cited.
Discussion of verbal and written argument
Course conclusion

Class 2
Teacher evaluations
Course evaluations

# CHAPTER ONE
## *UNDERSTANDING PERSUASION: THINKING LIKE A NEGOTIATOR*

TAKING A "WAR OF WORDS" TOO LITERALLY

1.  Instead of exploring the many facets of an issue, Tannen points out that the media prefers to make everything a battle. Controversy sells and conflict is interesting. The problem is that by assuming a polar position and defending it to the death, we close our ears to other points of view. It becomes a situation where everyone is talking and no one is listening anymore. Newspapers employ provoking and often adversarial headlines designed to stir up reader interest. Reporters endeavor to reveal all the hidden dirt on a public figure–rarely highlighting positive things the individual may have done. Class discussion may include a discussion regarding the Clinton scandals, Ken Starr, or political battles currently taking place in Congress.

    News media isn't the only culprit here. Most television talk shows feature adversarial confrontations like the one featured in Tannen's article. Shows like *The Jerry Springer Show* almost skip discussion entirely in favor of getting down to the physical blows. It would seem there is no room for middle ground as long as there is a market for fighting.

2.  By taking sides, we may block out any reasonable perspective the other side may present. In other words, we prevent consensus. Gun control could be one example. One side says ban all handguns (guns kill people), and the other says we have the constitutional right to bear arms (people kill people). Neither side wants to listen to the other, and very little progress has been made on the issue because no one is willing to give up any "ground."

3.  Student answers will vary.

4. Debate is often encouraged in many classrooms, especially in higher education. While the objective is usually to encourage discussion, argument is often the end result. The problem is that once arguments really get going, it is difficult to return the class to a more objective and thoughtful level. In some cases, students may become so angered at each other that shouting matches result. Tannen points out that this method of inquiry prevents productive discussion and eliminates the possibility for consensus.

The "winner-take-all" approach to arguments may prevent meaningful dialog. The inflexibility of this approach rarely solves the problem. In a situation where somebody "wins" and somebody "loses," there is bound to be resentment. In your effort to get your point across, you may forget the central issues and alternative viewpoints. Moreover, when one side feels that they have lost, they are unlikely to adopt the "winning" point of view anyway.

## SAMPLE ARGUMENTS FOR ANALYSIS

### THE CASE AGAINST TIPPING

1. Tipping has become an obligatory practice in which patrons are shamed or bullied into rewarding a service, no matter how good or poor that service is. Lewis wants to alert readers to this growing trend in our society, perhaps to motivate a change in behavior.

2. Lewis points out several reasons why tipping is bad. A) It may be abused by employers who will reduce wages in anticipation of the tip augmenting the employee's income. B) Tipping has its roots in "aristocratic conceit" in which the rich bestow money on those who serve them. C) It becomes so expected that some service people may retaliate when not given a good tip, regardless of the quality of service. D) The more expected a tip becomes, the less likely the server will work harder to earn it.

3. Lewis presents several examples from his own experience to support his claims. He starts his essay with the coffee shop/cup-on-the-counter scenario. He also presents the problems with New York City cab drivers. His examples may be considered a bit slanted because he does not account for situations in which stellar service should be rewarded. All of his examples present scenarios of little or poor service.

4. In his endeavor to present his argument, Lewis leaves little room for an alternative viewpoint. When he does "present" the opposite side, he is very negative. Using the phrase "offensively rich people may delight in peeling off hundred-dollar bills..." may not be fair to those individuals who approve tipping. It also questions the sincerity of people who are generous with their money. And comparing the taxi cab driver to the counter cup isn't exactly a parallel situation.

5. Peer group work.

THE CONSEQUENCES OF "CARNAGE AS ENTERTAINMENT"

1. Ellis believes that violent television and movies desensitize children to the realities of violence and encourages violent behavior. Ellis hopes to alert readers to this trend in our culture and correct it before it is too late.

2. Ellis provides reasons why we should be concerned about television violence. A) Children learn that extremely violent behavior, such as shooting one's classmates, receives extensive media coverage. They may get the idea that committing such acts will get them national attention and fame. B) Violent programming now dominates prime time television as well as film. C) Television violence is getting worse. D) Researches claim that there is a direct link between violence in the media and violent behavior in children.

3. Ellis uses the actual reports of school shooting to introduce his essay: five shootings in a seven-month period. He also presents statistical data regarding violence in television programming in paragraphs 10-12. Ellis may be making unfair comparisons.

   In the beginning of the article, he seems to imply that it is the news-coverage of the violent school shootings that encourages youth to commit violent acts operating under the belief that they will be "rewarded" fame and media coverage. He does not consider other reasons why youths may act out violent impulses. For most of the essay, he blames television programming and movies for violent trends. But are news reports of violence in the same category as violent movies?

4. Ellis expresses disbelief and outrage at the opposition's view. Specifically, he attacks Jack Valenti, president of the Motion Picture Association of America. He calls Valenti's opinion "irresponsible" leaving little doubt as to the writer's opinion of his opponents.

5. Peer group work.

## QUESTIONS FOR DISCUSSION AND WRITING

THE CASE AGAINST TIPPING

1. Student answers will vary.

2. Student answers will vary.


THE CONSEQUENCES OF "CARNAGE AS ENTERTAINMENT"

1. Student answers will vary.

2. Student answers will vary.

3. Ellis presents an "either-or" argument. He tells us that we must either fix the current problem, or face the end of civilization as we know it. Ellis is guilty of logical fallacy in that he provides little proof that media violence is truly going to cause the destruction of civilization. A better tactic may be simply to highlight the increase in violent behavior in children and suggest a correlation between this behavior and violent programming in the news, television programming, and films. He should also address other reasons for violent behavior in children, such as increased availability of firearms, drug use, peer pressure, and reduced parental guidance at home.

## CHAPTER END EXERCISES

1.
| | |
|---|---|
| a) arguable | b) arguable |
| c) not arguable | d) not arguable |
| e) arguable | f) arguable |
| g) not arguable | h) not arguable |
| i) arguable | j) not arguable |
| k) arguable | l) arguable |
| m) arguable | n) arguable |
| o) arguable | p) arguable |
| q) not arguable | r) arguable |

2. Student answers will vary.

3. Student answers will vary.

4. Student answers will vary.

# CHAPTER TWO
## *READING ARGUMENTS: THINKING LIKE A CRITIC*

1.
    a.  *ad hominem*
    b.  *non sequitur*, begging the question
    c.  slippery slope, *ad populum*
    d.  non sequitur
    e.  red herring and *ad homineum*
    f.  false analogy
    g.  *non sequitur*
    h.  circular reasoning
    i.  hasty generalization, and *post hoc, ergo propter hoc*
    j.  false analogy
    k.  stacking the deck
    l.  *ad populum*

# CHAPTER THREE
## *FINDING ARGUMENTS: THINKING LIKE A WRITER*

*There are no questions that need to be answered in this chapter for the Instructor's Manual.*

# CHAPTER FOUR
## *ADDRESSING ARGUMENTS: THINKING LIKE A READER*

### SAMPLE ARGUMENTS FOR ANALYSIS

DON'T FORGET THE SMOKERS

1. Author's Claims/Points: In our effort to prevent teenagers from smoking, we must not forget older smokers who still need our attention and assistance. Cigarettes are addictive. Tobacco companies know and count on this. Tobacco companies are trying to fight the FDA's regulation of cigarette marketing. The FDA's authority over tobacco must not be undermined.

2. Koop assumes the audience will understand the urgency of his message, and agree that cigarettes are bad for personal and public health. He also presumes that his audience understands some medical terminology, is fairly literate, and is informed of current political lobbying activities by the big tobacco companies.

3. Koop uses words like "Big Tobacco" and implies that tobacco companies are conspiring against the public health. He also accuses them of employing reverse psychology in their last campaign "against" teen smoking. He presents a very negative picture of his opponents, but does so in a very methodical and well-supported way. He tries to back up his claims with evidence the audience can relate to.

4. Koop is very respectful of his audience. He repeatedly employs inclusive words such as "we" and treats them like equals in his argument against big tobacco companies.

5. This argument is fairly balanced, although it does assume that the audience is of a like mind.

6.  Koop establishes common ground quite effectively. He appeals to his audience's desire to protect teens from the clutches of cigarettes and he comments that we should not abandon or forget smokers who want to quit. Both smokers and non-smokers are addressed without accusation or ill will.

7.  Koop hopes to enlighten his audience to the lobbying activities of "Big Tobacco."

## WHAT THE ANTISMOKING ZEALOTS REALLY CRAVE

1.  Author's Claims/Points: Antismoking advocates are infringing on the rights of smokers. Antismoking rhetoric should be more consistent and honest in admitting its objectives.

2.  Jacoby is writing *at* an audience of anti-tobacco supporters. At the same time, audience members who are smokers may feel included by knowing that he is defending their rights.

3.  Jacoby's argument is not very balanced. It is written from an angry viewpoint, and uses charged language. This is a "me against you" argument.

4.  Jacoby's attitude is belligerent and accusing. He is angry and not afraid to let his readers know it.

5.  This essay has many logical fallacies, including *ad hominem*, stacking the deck, red herrings and false analogies. Jacoby would have to alter the tone, style and structure of his argument to correct the problems with his editorial.

6.  Jacoby's intent is not to establish common ground, but perhaps to highlight some injustices surrounding the issue.

7.  The purpose of this essay is to address the inconsistencies in the anti-tobacco campaign, and highlight its unfair policies and prejudices.

## MEDIA HAVE FALLEN FOR THE MISGUIDED ANTISMOKING CAMPAIGN

1.  Author's Claims/Points: The media has succumbed to the view promoted by the popular antismoking campaign that smokers are victims lacking free will. Taxing smokers penalizes the poor. Teens are not smoking as much as we think, and hazards of second-hand smoke are questionable. Government, society and even the tobacco industry have abandoned the rights of smokers.

2.  Samuelson is addressing a largely neutral audience and assumes that he will be able to appeal to their sense of fairness. However, he perhaps assumes that they will not carefully examine his presentation of the "facts." This may assume a bit of naïveté on the part of his audience. His comment about cigarette taxation affecting the poor also assumes that they will be sympathetic to this issue.

3.  Samuelson tries to appear as if he is presenting a balanced view, but his interpretation and presentation of the data is skewed.

4.  Overall, Samuelson's tone is respectful of his audience.

5.  Samuelson is guilty of several logical fallacies including red herrings, stacking the deck, and non sequitur. For example, in his attempt to prove that studies give conflicting information, he mentions that in 1996, *only* 18.3 percent of teenagers smoked in the last month, a decrease since 1985. He ignores the fact that still almost 20% of teens smoked at all! He words this as if teen smoking is not a real problem. Another example is his comment that teens do a lot of bad things, so why are we singling out smoking. He is trying to direct the audience from the real issue that teens do smoke. He also withholds statistical data when it doesn't support his argument's goals.

6.  Common ground is established in Samuelson's appeal to the smoking poor, and his audience's sense of fairness.

7.  To redirect the media's coverage of smoking and to decrease bias in their reporting.

## CHAPTER END EXERCISES

1.  Student answers will vary.

2.  Reasons in favor of claim:
    a.  * Snowboarders tend to be young, reckless males who take risks.
        * Snowboarders jeopardize the slopes of family skiers.
        * Snowboarders tend to ski at extreme speeds, with little ability to slow themselves down.
    b.  * A 55-mile speed limit will reduce the number of fatal accidents.
        * A 55-mile speed limit allows for more reaction time.
        * A 55-mile speed limit nationwide takes the guesswork out of traveling on highways.
    c.  * Advertising condoms on television would help remove embarrassment associated with talking about them.
        * Advertising condoms on television would publicize their benefits.
        * Advertising condoms on television could help reduce STDs.
    d.  * Denying federal aid to students with drug convictions sends a clear message to young people of the ramifications of drug use.
        * The government shouldn't have to assist students who break the law.
        * Students will have a response to peer pressure "I can't, I could lose my loan."

Reasons to oppose claim:
  a.  * Snowboarding provides a good, athletic outlet for teens.
      * Snowboarders often stay on slopes specifically designated for that purpose.
      * Snowboarders exercise more caution because they know they are monitored closely by the ski patrol.
  b.  * A 55-mile speed limit is unrealistic, few people drive that slowly.
      * A 55-mile speed limit will increase commuting time.
      * A 55-mile speed limit may increase the number of traffic jams on highways.
  c.  *Advertising condoms on television may send the message that sexual promiscuity is permissible.
      * Advertising condoms on television may offend some people.
      * Advertising condoms on television could encourage teen experimentation.
  d.  * Students with a drug conviction shouldn't be penalized for what could be only one mistake.
      * Refusing federal aid could make students drop out of school; less educated people may be more likely to break to the law again.
      * Refusing federal aid to students in this category is too vague; isn't there a difference between a drug dealer and a teen who tries pot?

3. Student answers will vary.

4. Student answers will vary.

5. Connotations of words:
  a.  *Weird*: implies that something is odd or wrong with her choice.
      *Exotic*: of an intriguing nature and foreign in a positive way.
      *Unusual*: different from the expected, may be good or bad.
  b.  *Polluting*:  gives an impression of chemical and environmental dangers.
      *Stinking up*: a less formal, slang expression implying distaste.
      *Fouling*: a sense of toxicity, dangerous to health.

c.  *Unaware*: simply uninformed, doesn't know the facts.
    *Ignorant*: implies stupidity or lack of education.
    *Unconscious*: gives impression of obliviousness to one's surroundings.
d.  *Popular*: part of a movement approved by large group and in vogue.
    *Trendy*: a passing fad, not likely to last or without permanence.
    *Common*: part of an established way of thinking.
e.  *Stomped*: implies anger, hostility and some level of immaturity.
    *Marched*: seems purposeful, with determination.
    *Stepped*: she simply left.

6.

a. The rise of the news is personification. News is compared to a monster, an example of metaphor. The news monster "ate" the news industry, thus personifying this metaphor. Also, the situation is compared to a war, another metaphor. The term "airwaves" may be considered a dead metaphor, now part of common language.

b. The skin is creased *like* leather gloves–a simile.

c. Rodriquez feels (like) he was drowning, an example of a metaphor. The school baptizes its students into English, which is using personification. Also, Rodriguez says the sounds were ugly, the teacher's grip tender, and the conviction took--further examples of personification. The phrase "forced down my throat" is a personified metaphor that is also rather cliché.

d. Fiction is personified here by living, dying and providing.

e. The battle is compared to a holocaust, which is a metaphor. Also, the word holocaust had an original definition of destruction by fire or of sacrifice. The mass slaughter of European Jews during World War II was likened to a holocaust, so the word itself was once a metaphor.

f. The government is personified in this sentence by the word "step."

g.    Natural selection is personified as pushing buttons, endowing emotions, and coaxing choices. The phrase "push the buttons" is both a metaphor and a cliché.

7.  It is not that we are unconcerned with space exploration, it is that many Americans do not understand what these untold billions of dollars can accomplish.  While significant advances have been made in space research, we ask ourselves: Is life any safer?  Are material goods more abundant?  Has the expense extended our life expectancy or improved our overall health?  The answer is no.  Congressional leaders must realize that the nation's urgent problems of crime, homelessness, and unemployment are here on earth.  No government budget should be spared including NASA's.  While some people may object to cutbacks, they must remember that our tax dollars are limited. Overall, spending money on space exploration is wasteful.

# CHAPTER FIVE
## *SHAPING ARGUMENTS: THINKING LIKE AN ARCHITECT*

### QUESTIONS FOR DISCUSSION AND ANALYSIS

SCHOOLS CAN HELP TO PREVENT TEEN PREGNANCY

1. Martha identifies the problem after providing two paragraphs of statistical data and facts to support her claim. She begins by presenting the number of pregnancies in the US and the strain it puts on families, children, and taxpayers. She then states the problem outright in her third paragraph.

2. Martha proposes to solve the problem by implementing an interactive sex education program that encourages parents, teachers, and students to communicate openly. She begins to explain her plan in paragraph 4.

3. Martha touches on the different ways her idea will solve the problem in paragraphs 4 and 5, although she revisits her solution throughout the essay, effectively reminding her audience of her point.

4. In paragraph 7, Martha explains how she hopes her program will work by attacking the problem on two fronts rather than on only one.

5. While Martha admits that some people would object to her solution, she quickly explains that it is not an ideal world where all parents work together with their children. Until it is, we need sex education in the schools. The focus of her essay is not addressing the objections to her plan, but in proposing it.

6. Martha cites how other programs like hers were successful in California where teen pregnancies have dropped. She elaborates and provides statistics on their success in paragraph 7.

7. Martha conveys the mature attitude of a concerned parent. She accounts for alternative points of view, does not accuse any one party of negligence and focuses on problem solving.

**CHAPTER END EXERCISES**

Questions 1-8
Student answers will vary for this section.

# CHAPTER SIX
## *USING EVIDENCE: THINKING LIKE AN ADVOCATE*

## QUESTIONS FOR DISCUSSION AND ANALYSIS

RU 486: THE FRENCH ABORTION PILL AND ITS BENEFITS

1. Kelley argues that the abortion pill RU 486 should be made available to American women as a basic right. RU 486 will serve the public interest in reducing the number of unwanted pregnancies, and thus, she reasons, poverty levels. Kelley reasons that the pill is already available in many European countries, has been proven safe both in Europe and in FDA clinical trials, offers a non-surgical abortion option, provides for anonymity, and requires less recovery time. Kelley addresses her opposition briefly, by trying to persuade them with her definition of what constitutes life and living and with a socio-economic argument that RU 486 will reduce the number of welfare families.

2. Kelley's audience is probably young college age women between the ages of 18-25. In this age group herself, she addresses their fears and concerns about having children outside of marriage and "ruining" their lives and futures with a baby before they are emotionally and economically ready. She is addressing a primarily pro-choice audience, reinforced by her angry statements against the efforts of the anti-abortion movement to pressure the government and pharmaceutical companies into not making RU 486 available.

3. Kelley supports her argument with a variety of medical, social and personal resources. She cites *The New England Journal of Medicine* in several places to support her claims that the pill is safe and effective. She describes scenarios regarding the fears associated with and the difficulties of terminating a pregnancy. In this case, she draws primarily from social discourse. She also presents her own perspectives and opinions.

4. Some of Kelley's evidence is very reliable, such as the information drawn from *The New England Journal of Medicine* and Jacoby. This information describes the pill, its method of action, its efficacy, its side effects, and its safety. Likewise, her description of the social attitudes and stigma of abortion that many women face is also accurate. Kelley is less credible when she offers her opinions alone to support her argument. For example, her definition of life, while drawing from Thoreau, may be found faulty by many people. She certainly cannot speak for what the founding "Fathers [and Mothers]" believed life was, although she tries to do this. A more balanced discussion of life may improve this section. Kelley has also confused the Declaration of Independence with the Constitution. The Declaration of Independence is a proclamation of principles, but not a legal document guaranteeing certain rights and privileges. Using this document to support her argument may not be the best way to go.

5. Student answers will vary.

# CHAPTER SEVEN
## *ESTABLISHING CLAIMS: THINKING LIKE A SKEPTIC*

### FOR ANALYSIS AND DISCUSSION

FOR THE LOVE OF THE GAME

1. Spokas is advocating the random drug testing of Olympic athletes. She also feels that anabolic steroids give an unfair advantage to the athletes who use them, and this isn't what the Olympics "are supposed to be about." She does admit that such testing can be affected by birth control pills, but that, overall, it is necessary to even out the playing field.

2. Spokas cites examples of medal-winning athletes who used steroids, such as Ben Johnson and the athletes from East Germany. She also describes the ways athletes try to beat the current system, which employs planned drug testing of winners after the competition. She further details the Olympic motto, which she uses to support her concept of the Olympic spirit of competition.

3. Spokas taps into the popular feeling (ad populum) that the Olympics are about fair competition. The winners of Olympic competition are supposed to represent the finest natural athletes of that sport. There is also a perception Olympic athletes are the embodiment of skill, determination, and wholesomeness. Drugs detract from this Olympic image and message.

4. Student answers will vary.

5. Spokas' use of qualifiers allow her to acknowledge some of her opponents' concerns, while downplaying the concern at the same time. It is interesting to note that she does not use these qualifiers in many of her own warrants. For example, in paragraph 7, she says "Random testing *will* make it *impossible* for athletes...to cheat..." She also says, "It *will force* them to reduce if not abandon taking anabolic steroids..." Readers may take issue with such sweeping statements.

6. Spokas' entire article is a rebuttal itself. She is *arguing against* the idea that testing athletes at prearranged and announced testing times is a more reliable and proper testing method than random testing.

## ARGUING FOR INFANTICIDE

1. Kelley claims that despite his prior belief that abortion would not cause an overall devaluation of human life, Pinker's article, printed in an intellectual media resource (*The New York Times*) indicates that it indeed has. He then proceeds to explain what was wrong with Pinker's claims and support.

2. Pinker claims that infanticide, in cases such as those recently publicized by the media, are not as morally horrible as we think. Many cultures accept infanticide. Furthermore, mothers instinctually weigh the overall "survival" prospects of the infant when deciding whether to let it live or die. Kelley objects to Pinker's references from "moral philosophers" regarding what makes one human, his hypothesis on how the mind works, and his argument's support by Michael Tooley. Kelley attacks Tooley's reasoning and thus, that of Pinker as well.

3. Kelley largely disregards Pinker's comments on the actions of a few "depressed new mothers" to compare their actions to that of "millions of mothers." This allows Kelley to focus on the "monstrosity" of Pinker's claim. However, Kelley's omission may actually skip a point he should have addressed–that the action of depressed new mothers is

one of the mother's perception of her own survival, not that of the infant's.

4. Kelley implies that the legalization of abortion has caused an intellectual and moral shift in American culture typified by the opinions of people such as Pinker. If Pinker, a respected scientist, believes this, and *The New York Times*, a respected newspaper, prints it, then it must represent the opinions of a larger population.

5. Kelley's use of words here indicates that he may believe that Pinker is leaving himself an out. By rewording Pinker's warrant this way, he implies to the audience that this is *exactly* what Pinker was advocating.

6. Euphemizing something means you make it sound less harsh, such as saying "she passed away" instead of "she died." Kelley proposes that Pinker took the basic ideas from Tooley's article and made them sound less harsh. This means that Pinker embraces the same ideas as Tooley, he just prettified the language. Kelley reinforces the connection between Pinker and the more radical Tooley by pointing out that Pinker does indeed quote Tooley in his article. Pinker may not actually endorse Tooley's theories, but Kelley makes it sound like he does.

7. Student answers will vary.

8. Student answers will vary.

# CHAPTER EIGHT
## *RESEARCHING ARGUMENTS: THINKING LIKE AN INVESTIGATOR*

*There are no questions that need to be answered in this chapter for the Instructor's Manual.*

# CHAPTER NINE
## *GENDER MATTERS*

## BEING FEMALE: WHAT IS IT LIKE TO BE A WOMAN TODAY?

SAPLINGS IN THE STORM

1. Pipher uses this analogy to emphasize her claim that adolescent girls in America become vulnerable and eventually "lost" as they conform to cultural perceptions. Have students locate places in the text where Pipher employs this analogy and discuss the before and during adolescence behaviors of girls. Ask students to think of times when they too have lost or pushed aside their "authentic selves" due to cultural pressures and then ask them to share how they "resurfaced."

2. Student answers may vary, but direct them to the three factors Pipher states "make young women vulnerable." If students do think girls must make sacrifices to socially fit in, have them elaborate on *what* is sacrificed and *how* that sacrifice leads to peer acceptance.

3. Pipher feels "androgynous adults are the most well adjusted." Have students make separate lists of the behaviors androgynous girls and boys would benefit from to highlight their prescribed notions of gender roles; note the differences and ask how the transition from adolescence to adulthood might further change these and why.

4. One way of having students see if Pipher's article is of universal application is for them to isolate one paragraph and replace the word "girls" with "boys." In thinking of parent-child relationships and corporate America's influence, the gender of an adolescent might not matter, but what issues that Pipher brings up are solely in relation to girls? Have students debate the issue of perceptions and images to note any differences in opinion that are gender-based.

5. Have students first define the intended audience of this piece. If it does not include men, ask them what parts of the piece could be considered general concerns for adolescents, then speculate on what Pipher's *male* clients' issues might be. If she had included some adolescent male issues, how would her thesis be different? Return to question number one and ask students to consider if and how adolescent *boys* "disappear mysteriously into the Bermuda Triangle."

6. Lead students through brief descriptions of gender stereotypes of the 1930s, 1950s, etc., noting national concerns of the time periods. Ask students to note Pipher's examples of Michelle, Holly, and Gail and then to place these three girls' problems into the different historical contexts. Discuss how the underlying social pressures facing these girls have changed according to each decade and how Pipher's advice to them might change also.

## THE INDEPENDENT WOMAN AND OTHER LIES

1. Discussion of the title of Roiphe's piece can begin by having students identify the words that connote a "lie," which should lead them to paragraph 2 and the word "façade." Answering "Why" such words and ideas are "lies" will require students to consider if they can accept the ironies and contradictions that Roiphe discusses, such as the "refined version of the double standard."

2. Guide students through the paragraphs that cite examples and critique each one on its effectiveness as support to her claim. Ask them to consider the fact that most of her examples are either of friends of hers or pop theorists on the issue. Are these reliable sources? Why or why not? This can lead into a debate on the universality of the issue.

3. Explaining the term "rape fantasy" may raise students' eyebrows, but its use as an analogy does parallel the "man in the gray flannel suit" as both configure women desiring men in power positions over them.

4. Student answers will vary.

5. Student answers will vary.

IN THE COMBAT ZONE

1. Have students seek Silko's answers to these questions, but extend the discussion to ask them for their personal answers to them as well. Do they agree or disagree with Silko's claims?

2. Student answers will vary. If the majority disagree with Silko's father's comment, ask them what they feel could equalize the differences between men and women.

3. Defining patriarchy can stem from a discussion of gender role stereotypes. What are "traditional" male and female roles? A discussion of what feminism is should also supplement remarks on patriarchy. How does the issue of one gender assuming it has more power transfer into physical acts of violence? Remind students to focus on violence from strangers toward women, not domestic violence.

4. Have students reflect on each of the five rapists described in terms of power. How could they scale them in such terms, i.e., which do they think had the most desire for power and why?

5. Students can explore what their feelings are about women who can defend themselves and why these two male groups might fear such women in their lives. With respect to the application of this statement to American society, have students define American belief systems in terms of gender relations. Then consider what the differences would be for women living in rural and urban regions of the country since Silko gives examples of potential acts of violence upon her in both settings.

6. First ask students what they understand Silko's thesis to be. Ask students what the main point of this example is to see what support it offers to that thesis, then ask them to consider how the essay might read if this example were deleted.

7. Considering all of the examples Silko offers to justify women's use of firearms, guide students through the metaphors she creates, e.g., who/what is hunted and by whom?

## BEING MALE: WHAT IS IT LIKE TO BE A MAN TODAY?

## HOW U.S. SCHOOLS ARE STIFLING MALE STUDENTS

1. Have students identify the sources Pollack cites to see if his claims follow a deductive framework. Is his use of educational reports and studies together with psychological and health research effective? Why or why not?

2. Student answers will vary. Could students agree with his connection if Pollack had brought up *non-violent* acts?

3. An opportunity for collaborative work: have students work together to identify the author's solutions and recommendations to schools and then propose their own depending on the injustices they see. What do they think currently works in schools to "serve the boys," and what would be their ideal school situation to defer unequal treatment between boys and girls?

4. Have students discuss the assumptions this statement makes about educators and schools. Ask them what their most "captivating" classroom experiences have been and how, if at all, their gender influenced that way of learning.

5. Building on the answers in question 4, now have students debate on *what* boy and girl learning styles are; how separation could benefit a learning process; and how it could not. Does the subject material of the class matter since Pollack himself brings up the sciences, reading and writing?

6. Students might discuss what standards they have been exposed to thus far in their education and which of these have been unfair in terms of gender. In thinking of their own experiences concerning when and if flexibility was offered, was it enjoyed by one gender more than the other? How so?

## THE MEN WE CARRY IN OUR MINDS

1. Have students identify passages where Sanders tells his readers of the environment in which he was raised. Vivid descriptions describe a place where men endured lives of labor and physical hardship and where women were more involved in school and community affairs. Because women's lives seemed to him more expansive and free than those of men, he finds it easier to identify the injustice inflicted on minorities such as native Americans than to understand the deprivation women have suffered.

2. Student answers will vary, but based on the impression Sanders has of the lives of women as those of more leisure (see question 1), it seems that yes he does feel they are the privileged class. Have students discuss if they perceive him to have changed his mind since his college days now that he surely has encountered these higher-educated, upper-class women in the professional world.

3. Open for discussion and debate. An interesting strategy might be for students to adopt the positions of the women mentioned (both the upper-educated *and* the women from his hometown) and then have them switch to adopt Sanders' male viewpoint. How might these different socio-economic perspectives respond to one another? Students may point out that each group discussed might have experiences that do not support Sanders' stereotypes.

4. The essay would read more like a factual report on the relationship between men and women. Have students highlight the first-person sections that were most effective to catching their attention and discuss the rhetorical strategy of using personal anecdotes to make one's readers more sympathetic, persuaded, motivated, angry, etc. Since Sanders is such a good example of this strategy, ask students to imitate his style in a future writing assignment or to recall instances when they have used personal anecdotes in their writing. How did they go about picking their examples? How, then, do they think Sanders went about picking his?

5. Have students consider the unstated expectations for males and females and what Anneke's statement means in those terms. Is being a victim the same as assuming the passive role in a relationship? Do students think Sanders and Anneke think it is more "traditional" or OK for a *woman* to take the passive role (and be taken care of) than for a male? Why?

6. Students should first identify who Sanders' audience would be (remind them of his book) and then they can discuss the effect of Anneke's comments on *their* reading of the essay. If this female point of view was not given, would his argument be weaker or somehow stronger? Would the women at his college make such a comment?

# IS MALE POWER REALLY A MYTH? A FIRST GLANCE

1. Student answers will vary, but be certain Farrell's definition of power is addressed since his views seem to address the different kinds of power exercised depending on the relationship.

2. Student answers will vary. Consider discussing if nationalism during a world war is even comparable to the "battle" he seems to be envisioning between men (or the expectations of men) and women.

3. Student answers will vary.

4. Student answers will vary.

5. Ask student to define "anti-power" by referring to the text, particularly the phrase "your job as a man" and then the words "deference and subservience." Consider the Steve Petrix example in reverse and have students ponder if the marriage relationship and home setting play more significant roles in the reactions. Perhaps if the two were not married nor in a relationship, would the reactions have been the same? What point is Farrell trying to make about *husbands* "having" to be bodyguards? Do students think his point is applicable to single men too?

## CONAN AND ME

1. Persky sets up a standard for a heroic male response to crisis earlier in the second paragraph by describing an *ideal* male reaction. His actual confrontation with the intruder juxtaposes the desire to play that ideal with his actual reaction to real-life fear and terror. This says something about gender stereotypes, e.g., male as protector, and their effect on the behavior and attitudes of people in everyday life. Discussion might expose the difficulty of living up to such expectations—and the resultant need for hiding traits that do not conform with these gender stereotypes.

2. Student answers will vary, but also ask students to reflect upon when they have hidden themselves from the world and why they feel they might have had that reaction. Was it due to gender in any way?

3. These clues serve to identify the audience Persky is writing for: he uses them to position himself as a man, just like any other as an active participant in pop culture, vulnerable to the pains and triumphs of cultural sex-role conditioning. The first clues are most obvious: the comparison of himself to a combination of Arnold Schwartzenegger and his mother. Upon confrontation, Persky says he is reading *The Bonfire of the Vanities*, a popular book representing the lives of hard-hitting New York lawyers and businessmen whom the book's author calls "Masters of the Universe." Next, he considers drawing upon the "new, upperbody strength" developed at the "Vertical Club," implying a kind of artificiality in the current mania for health clubs. Each of these clues is familiar enough to allow for reader recognition and identification.

4. Student answers will vary. Ask students to state Persky's argument (if this has not already been established), and if their responses show they identify with his feelings, do they agree with his argument more?

5. Persky's introduction is an apt way of getting at the complicated issue of cultural affectation and concealed identities. The Reiner anecdote is also a good way to set the tone for the piece, which is informal, chatty, occasionally bemused, and written as a first-person narrative. Have students discuss what their answers were for the "As You Read" section for this piece and ask them to identify the other places throughout the story that Persky, through his own sense of humor, makes himself accessible to his reader.

## MR. FIX-IT AND THE HOME-IMPROVEMENT COMMITTEE

1. Have students compare the first two paragraphs of the essay with the last two paragraphs to summarize Gray's intentions. In terms of hearing if students agree with his conclusions, neutrally break up the classroom into Martians and Venusians. Do students find that his separation of the problems and needs of men and women is too simplistic?

2. Building off of the first exercise, a teacher can now use the imaginary planets in his/her classroom to try to get the planets to come to a consensus as Gray has the planets in his examples do. Obviously, there will be differing opinions, with some surely not gender-based, but have students return to the essay to examine how Gray writes his way to a consensus.

3. Gray's ability to tap in to the feelings of both sexes helps to establish his argument more effectively as he devotes an equal amount of explanation to each. Regarding if this is the "best" technique, ask students to consider who the buyers of Gray's book are and if they think his readership is made up of a relatively equal amount of men and women. If not, although his television appearances have been mainstream news-oriented shows that appeal to both sexes, why do they feel Gray's work attracts one gender more than the other? While Gray does bring up the complaints of both sexes, the idea that females verbalize their feelings more might factor into a larger female readership.

4. Student answers will vary, but probe to see if students remain "loyal" to the planets they were assigned in class, or if they relish in the opportunity to switch planets.

5. Ask students to analyze Gray's language use to see if it reveals his gender. If the point of Gray's article is to have both sexes recognize their differences (or complaints), how did he also remain a neutral voice of authority? Remembering that he is a psychologist, do students feel he may have overanalyzed aspects of male-female relations?

6. Student answers will vary, but these opinions can lead to intense discussion regarding how males and females communicate with each other.

## I'M SORRY, I WON'T APOLOGIZE

1. Student answers will vary, but also have them think of examples of their own when an apology was not given. Was it due to the pride of one's gender?

2. America's tendency to not apologize is one that may or may not lead to cultural resistance since America is the leading world power. However, the tendency to not apologize could have significant effects *within* America. Tannen points out in paragraph eleven that those imprisoned for offenses sometimes never say they are sorry, from which one could presume they would become repeat offenders; therefore, no contrition, increased crime rates. Besides criminals, American society as a whole would increasingly become less democratic and more self-centered due to the lack of "I'm sorry's."

3. Many of the points Tannen makes are applicable to the Clinton apology. Take for instance her remark in paragraph twelve, "Apologies seem to come most easily from those who know their error was unintentional." Students could debate over whether his affair and subsequent cover-up was intentional.

4. Student answers will vary.

5. Thinking about Segal's quote will lead students to contemplate the term "unconditional love." Segal seems to be saying that if people love each other unconditionally, then they will automatically forgive everything—but is this really the case in relationships between friends, family members, and spouses? Tannen's revision of the phrase might be more realistic by today's standards, so student's responses may evoke such attitudes.

## IN EACH OTHER'S COMPANY

1. Once students have made such lists, have them collaborate in groups to revise lists (add items and re-word others) and then present them to each other to compare and discuss the basis for the lists—socialization or biology. Since socialization factors will most likely be the foundation of their lists, try to elicit what biological factors could bring about "obvious differences" between friendships?

2. Consider why readers are given the detail that Bill is a concert promoter. Does this mean he relies on communication more than Gold's other friends? Throughout the entire essay there is a juxtaposition of action versus communication. This could be a reason why Gold makes his request, and if women's friendships are considered less physically active, the likelihood of them making such a pact is lessened. However, remind students that this latter point is of Gold's making and not a universal thread of female friendships.

3. Gold's support is primarily personal anecdotes and his credibility as a published interviewee on "male bonding." He also focuses on a select group of men—divorced fathers. This limits his views on relationships as it suggests men only have friendships with other men when they do not have women in their lives. To dispute Gold's limited views, students may reflect upon the male-male, male-female, and/or female-female friendships they have had throughout their lives in school or who they have "bonded" with most closely to note if gender consciously or unconsciously affected such bonds.

4. Besides the "un-male" action of kissing fellow male friends, it seems Gold is more upset by the fact that his friend did not understand his points about self-love. Gold also accuses his friend of getting caught up in the "politically correct feminist notion," which he feels is not relevant to their discussion of male friendships.

5. Again, this question refers to the action versus communication aspect of male-male friendships. Students should return to the adjectives they noted as they read to determine why a male author would make such a statement. If racquetball is a test of physical endurance, how is it also a builder of male friendships?

THE COMFORT OF FRIENDS

1. Throughout her essay, Quindlen notes that her female friendships are based in verbal communication, which is "probing and intimate" while men's are "skin deep" (paragraph three). Have students discuss their opinions regarding verbal communication in their friendships and then direct them to Quindlen's final sentence, "We talk, therefore I am." Have they ever experienced the fulfillment Quindlen has by talking to their friends and did the gender of the friend(s) make a difference?

2. Student answers will vary.

3. Quindlen's reference to a "man's-woman" classifies women who see other women as competition for men, but students might also consider this term to describe women who are like men in that they exhibit strong competitive natures in all pursuits.

4. Students may find that because she talks and depends on talking to this circle of friends that Quindlen's friends are similar, but point out to them that each provides "a sympathetic ear" from a different perspective and/or frequency. Such a close analysis of the circle of friends will also evoke some of John Gray's ideas about Mars and

Venus in that Quindlen's friends do not offer directions or immediate suggestions for improvement.

5. Again, these comparisons highlight Quindlen's claim of the importance of talking to learn about yourself and your world. In terms of playground behavior for girls, *conversation* is a contact sport. This is something Quindlen now sees in her daughter's life and hopes for her son.

6. The "sad" aspect of men's friendships to Quindlen's friend is that their emotional and professional lives (or what they perceive these lives *should* be) would never let them drop everything to comfort a friend diagnosed with a sickness, nor would they "laugh, cry and talk and talk and talk" together for a whole weekend. The traditional view is that men are not nurturers or sensitive enough to console someone in such a situation, again returning to the thesis that men's friendships are skin deep and not based in verbal communication (even Herbert Gold half-heartedly remarks, "Talk may not be as true as racquetball, but discussion can sometimes arrive at understanding"). Have students debate the issue.

# CHAPTER TEN
## *RACE AND ETHNICITY*

## IDENTITY AND STEREOTYPES: CAN WE MOVE BEYOND LABELS?

### A WOMAN FROM HE-DOG

1.  Paragraphs 2-6 detail the difficulties of being an American Indian woman. The acts committed upon these women prove that they have been taken advantage of and not taken seriously. Refer students to these and other moments in the text that account gender difficulties as a woman and racial ones as an Indian. Can they ever be separated?

2.  Using the examples from the text to answer question 1, the privileges she associates with white males are made blatantly obvious. They are the ones who have the power to take advantage of the weaker minority, i.e., the American Indian woman. Have students attempt to make a list of privileges white males have that other races/genders do not have. This may cause students to find holes in her argument since these privileges oftentimes do extend to others (via physical and intellectual powers, etc.).

3.  Brave Bird's account is one of a person searching for an identity that is "real" or does not have to be fought for. As noted by her role at the second Wounded Knee, she is a woman of strength who deserves the unstated recognition given to white men everyday. Her choice of the word "louse" seems appropriate since she explains her dilemma with being a lighter-skinned Indian; however, she does mention that she would fight with those who called her "an iyeska, a breed." Students might acknowledge that she has used her physical power to oppress (albeit fellow Native Americans) just as she has been oppressed, which would then weaken her argument.

4. Besides to offer a female opinion from a rarely heard culture, Brave Bird's account is trying to give readers an inside look at the life of a Sioux. She notes the accomplishments and struggles her tribe has survived to show that its members are just as powerful and deserving of a life free of oppression as anyone else. Again using the examples of difficulties American Indians face (question 1), students can now discuss why she included all of these and not just the ones of her own personal plight.

5. Refer students to paragraphs 3, 6, and 20 and open the class to discussion as to why her repetition of the phrase is used and if it works to her advantage in making her argument.

6. Ask students to work in groups to come up with their own definitions of "alien" and how that definition can be associated with the phrase "more powerful." Brave Bird considers white society in America as a culture different than her own because it is the majority. Along with defining "alien" can come the idea of conforming and imposing. Her account tells of white males as persons of power who have tried to take control over her people; ask students if they feel the whites Brave Bird describes were trying to assimilate the Indians and have them deny their race or were they trying to eliminate them?

7. Brave Bird's recounting of her tribe's history in paragraphs 10-16 adds credibility to her points because it offers readers the viewpoint from a perspective they most probably have not heard from before. She, personally, gains credibility as a survivor of Wounded Knee and her story's opening could be seen as testament for women, single mothers, and their children.

# COLORBLIND

1. Student answers will vary but discussion of other myths/stereotypes can be used to spark discussion. For example, a "common" myth created by race is the lasting one that the white race is the only one who can gain power positions, which is seen in American government, media, etc.

2. Fabricated cultural perceptions of race offer no room to collaborate and synthesize power. As alluded to in question 1, there is the idea that one group has the power while the others are oppressed. Another myth that persists from generational perceptions is that whomever we learn as children to be in the power position keeps that role. As long as these misguided cultural perceptions continue, there seems no way of changing or denying the myth to future generations, resulting in severed communication ties between races. Ask students to reflect on myths they have heard and if/when their views were changed by oral or written communication between races.

3. The example of Eric McGinnis offers, among other myths, the topic of interracial dating as a means for Kotlowitz to discuss a community geographically separated by race. But before his discussion of McGinnis, at the end of paragraph 4 Kotlowitz states "We—blacks and whites—need to examine and question our own perspectives. Only then can we grasp each other's myths and grapple with the truths." It does not seem that the extended example of the McGinnis case offers a means to do this. Ask students to examine, as the suggestion for "As You Read" stated, who the author quotes to see if he suggests ways these people examined and questioned their perspectives. Otherwise he is just offering commentary on a problem he himself has already recognized instead of using this example to offer recommendations for getting these two towns to "grapple" with each other.

4. Student answers will vary but remind them of the social and geographical positions of power that exist and the "majority rules"

concept which can transcend notions of racial power. For instance, any race might feel a sense of urgency or discomfort, whether it be physical or non-physical, in an environment not dominated by those of one's race.

5. Kotlowitz's conclusion enforces the myth that "even the best of people have already chosen sides" a generalization that perpetuates the racial separation he opposes. In paragraph 15, he remarks that he finds it easy to talk to blacks, yet he does not quote the Benton Harbor schools superintendent in paragraph 12 whom he says, "made no effort to hide his contempt for the white power structure." Direct students to these passages and ask them to find others that are ironic considering his intended aims.

6. Building off of the answers to question 5, teachers can now isolate paragraph 15 to highlight the roles the race of Ben Butzbaugh and Renee Williams play in this example.

THE MYTH OF THE LATINA WOMAN: I JUST MET A GIRL NAMED MARIA

1. Feeling like an "other" is universal, but Ortiz Cofer's argument offers sound examples of the differences between Puerto Rican and "white" cultures. Most evident are the ones that revolve around fashion, but direct students to her statement in paragraph 1, "Oh that British control. How I coveted it" which hints at a difference in demeanor. Also, paragraph 4 ends with a comparison between Puerto Rican festivities and American parties.

2. Begin by asking students to determine what America's cultural ideology is and what is considered mainstream. Other than Hispanic cultures, students should consider the problems other cultures may face due to heritage and geographic history.

3. Student answers will vary but ask them to recall movies and music they have seen or heard that portray Latina women as seductive temptresses. Have they seen anything in the media that has *not* offered that image?

4. The island system of morality centered life around family and religion, predominantly Catholicism. These customs liberated young girls to feel free to wear what they wanted to show off and celebrate the bodies God gave them, but then restrained them as their over-protective brothers made sure to limit the responses to such provocative displays (paragraph 6). This leads to misunderstandings when the island culture is removed to a foreign and less understanding environment that holds different ideological values.

5. Ortiz Cofer's poem at the end of her essay reinforces her claim that while different races/cultures with different customs do speak to each other, they have not fully realized that their languages are not exactly the same.

6. As "one of the lucky ones" Ortiz Cofer attributes her fortune to her family's incentive to allow her to advance her education and travel. Ask students if they feel this statement excludes Puerto Ricans who will never have a "public life," and if so, do they feel Ortiz Cofer's points to be weakened. Has she denied her culture in any way by calling herself a "lucky one"?

WHO IS A WHIZ KID?

1. Thinking about editors' jobs as ones that try to exclude bias, Gup was probably surprised that this supposed neutral voice was using a classificatory "them." The quote also suggests Asian Americans have been excluded from reportage thus far.

2.  As the evidence in his article suggests, reactions from parents and teachers may be different as they may place a burden on children to succeed in areas not natural to them. These stereotypes that Gup mentions also prove the divisions among races today. Ask students to think about how these races could converse with one another without preconceived notions about each other.

3.  Gup claims individuality is denied when stereotypes are assumed as reality. They become representative of the race rather than people seeing individuals as products of their parents' influences and personal commitment (paragraph 6).

4.  Ask students first to discuss what they know about inner city conflicts and then try to come to an agreement or disagreement with Gup's comment.

5.  Offer students an overview of Hitler's viewpoints regarding the power of the German race and the wars and horror it led to all over Europe. Although students may not recognize the myth to be active today, discuss the prejudices, if any, Jews still face.

6.  Student answers will vary.

FREE AT LAST? A PERSONAL PERSPECTIVE ON RACE AND IDENTITY IN AMERICA

1.  As Loury states in paragraph 3, racial identity is a social and cultural more than a biological construct; therefore, Woody's middle class and suburban "look" is typical of whites. The opinions on why Woody culturally identifies himself as black may vary but could stem from an allegiance to his grandparents' heritage. Or it could be that Woody wishes to identify himself with that part of him that seems the most distinct.

2. Considering the author's use of "passing" as something not favorable, he also suggests Woody's desire to be accepted as black was "in atonement for his parents' sins," perhaps with passing seen as the sin. It becomes important to him because he wants to correct his parents' wrongs.

3. Not vouching for his friend showed disloyalty to his race, and serves as the springboard for Loury's recognition of the combination of race and personal identity. Not vouching for a friend, no matter what race, can become a haunting memory, so Loury's use of his story here works to emphasize his argument that people should create their own identities from experiences instead of cultural perceptions.

4. Have students adopt the positions of Loury and Woody and discuss the implications of "passing" to both. Which is more likely to relish in the idea of a shared racial and social experience?

5. Accepting a socially constructed ethnic identity causes one to continue the line of misguided relations with other races as Loury's own experience with his sons has come to remind him.

6. Open to discussion.

## UNITY AND DIVERSITY: CAN THEY EXIST TOGETHER?

THE RETURN OF THE MELTING POT

1. The more liberal culture of America these days accepts and seems to advocate diversity and individuality as a means to success and this is what Schlesinger supports with his revision to the national currency slogan "e pluribus unum."

2. Student answers will vary but construct debates for and against the idea of a group self-esteem.

3. Responses can return to the "e pluribus unum" reference as America paradoxically considers itself a unified place of freedom and democracy. Schlesinger's use of the example emphasizing the importance of Irish Americans assimilating into mainstream culture agrees with his argument that a culture first ingest its own and then explore, rather than argue its way in to the mainstream via "turgid" facts.

4. Schlesinger supports this statement by going beyond the historical events of immigrants first moving here to explain a current society that does demonstrate its own experiences. Direct students to paragraph 18 where "Western democratic tradition in its true proportions" is described because it reminds us that when Europeans first settled here, they did not know what the proportions were.

5. Student answers will vary but have them share experiences with each other in class discussion.

## A DIFFERENT MIRROR (EXCERPT)

1. Takaki's introduction works to prove that today there are many Americans with limited views of the ethnicities in their own country. By offering this example, the author sets up his commentary on the "racial divide" in America and his credentials to offer ways to correct it.

2. Paragraph 9 offers some well-known examples of racial violence. The "racial crisis" alludes to the inability to address such conflict through reasoned communication. Takaki uses this term to comment on how awareness of other cultures' and races' beliefs can be learned in a system of multicultural education, which can then diminish the future chances for conflict.

3. Bloom and Hirsch are discussed as authors who discuss the ramifications of whites becoming the minority. Takaki's views on

their work may not come off as fair by way of the language he uses to introduce their points, for example, "perplexity" and "worry" about diversity.

4. Takaki offers detailed mini-chronicles of the experiences of African Americans, Asian Americans, Chicanos, Irish, Jews, and Indians. Group students and ask them to be representatives of these perspectives to hear their explanations of social identification and resistance.

5. Building off of the previous exercise, have students review Takaki's analysis. Develop a position on the assigned race and its antithesis. Note the similarities that may arise from this discussion. For example, how is each race individually pitted against labor economics and then each other?

6. Students answers will vary and may note that this omission reinforces Schlesinger's admission that historians' objective is critical analysis and not necessarily to advance multicultural instruction.

## DIVERSITY AND ITS DISCONTENTS

1. It seems Madrid's examples of locations like Peru and Pakistan are exotic because one does not hear of them everyday—not as many immigrants have come from those countries. And although Madrid is an American without immediate family in exotic locations, he still classifies himself as "other" because of his name, physical appearance, and speech patterns (paragraph 2).

2. In paragraph 5 Madrid states, "School was where one became American." In school, ideas of uniformity as acceptance pervaded through socialization and discipline, and it is likely school administrators and teachers unconsciously created this myth with the goal of creating a school that ran smoothly. It is a myth after all for the

same reasons Madrid calls himself "other,"--appearance plays a more significant role in acceptance.

3. Unlike "academic protectionism" which considers curriculum for students, "intellectual protectionism" refers to the hiring and subsequent treatment of professional academics in a university. Ethnicity should not be an issue, but it is and Madrid brings up this aspect of the multicultural education debate. The impact on students would be that respected professors from varied cultural backgrounds could be seen as role models to students of all races and backgrounds as well as educators offering new perspectives to their field of study.

4. Americans of a city and not a village atmosphere are undeniably different, which is what the pastor is pointing out to Madrid's grandmother. Ask students if they find this story disturbing considering the idea that such non-acceptance would happen in a place of religious worship. Also, the fact that the pastor warns Madrid's grandmother of such a possibility suggests that such behavior may have already happened.

5. & 6. Both questions ask students to reflect upon Madrid's definitions of these words and can be taken as an opportunity for groupwork. Students can discuss Madrid's definitions and grapple for meaning with each other in order to advance their own.

*Bilingual Education: Does it alienate or assimilate?*

LOCO, COMPLETAMENTE LOCO

1. Considering the details given in this example, it is likely that students will agree that it is effective and credible. It offers a then and now picture of Rosa's opinions and reactions to bilingual education for her children. It also demonstrates that her daughter triumphed in a non-bilingual school system.

2.  The variety of examples given are from states all over the United States, not just California, which supports Garvin's points that bilingual education is not just a "border" issue; it is a *national* problem.

3.  Student opinions will vary, but Rosa's example demonstrates this economic ramification of not having mastered the English language. She and her husband were not forced to learn the language as baby-sitters or busboys, jobs that earned them (parents) below the minimum wage.

4.  The tone is at times hostile, but always persuasive and effective. Readers sense the parents' anger described as well as Garvin's strong feelings against bilingual education. For instance, refer students to the comparison of bilingual education enterprise as a "multi-billion dollar hog trough" and gauge their reactions to this word choice.

5.  Have students debate the two sides that this statement represents: whether parents know best or whether educators know best. Since little is told of what it is that bilingual educators do, what kind of training do students suspect? Does this training make these educators better judges of what is best for children?

6.  Student answers will vary although the idea of group presentations may work to have students organize and balance their thoughts.

## BILINGUALISM: OUTDATED AND UNREALISTIC

1.  After reading the whole essay students may also recognize that the last paragraph reinforces this first claim since it states that Hispanics who favor bilingual education are seeking admission from the "gringo" that Spanish is a valuable presence and deserves to be learned alongside English.

2. Remembering his own story, Rodriguez feels that Hispanic children are giving up symbols of home in the middle class classroom. The price of adulthood is that they will recall their education as a complete separation from or betrayal of their home culture.

3. As indicated by the questions for Garvin's article, he uses a variety of opinions to support his argument against bilingual education. While Rodriguez's argument is similar, his essay is more directed to Hispanic opinions of bilingual education. His example of a Latvian man "forcing himself to relinquish the 'luxury' of reading books in Russian" does not seem as relevant although students could see its relation to his closing views of the price children of immigrants enrolled in a bilingual curriculum pay.

4. From what has been explained about bilingual education programs, one can infer that these programs are offered at public schools where students are probably of lower economic standing. In terms of his discussion of prospective jobs for immigrant children, Garvin would agree with this perspective that bilingualism is a class issue.

5. According to Rodriguez, the "dirty little secret" is that Hispanics who favor bilingual education are doing so out of self-promotion. They believe there is an easy way for themselves to be public and private without consequences. Ask students if they feel such a balance is possible for any race.

6. Asking students to isolate this paragraph and analyze it for its effectiveness brings readers back to Rodriguez's main intention—to argue against bilingual education in Hispanic communities. To Rodriguez, the parents and educators become content while the "dark-eyed children" lose out. Ask students what their first impressions of this paragraph were since its sentence structure and word choice simultaneously summarize and persuade.

# LET'S NOT SAY ADIOS TO BILINGUAL EDUCATION

1. After defining the term xenophobic for students, refer students back to paragraphs 25-30 of Garvin s article. If looked at from the administrative point of view, could these situations have been rooted in dislike for foreigners? Also, have students isolate paragraph 30 of Garvin and then pit its percentage against Rovira's opening paragraph's claims.

2. Open to discussion. Although Rovira inserts this comment about other languages (also refer students to a similar one at the end of paragraph 15), her support and examples are limited to Miami and California where Spanish is the second language predominantly included in a bilingual education curriculum. Ask students if they can consider Rovira an advocate of bilingual education for all languages with just these two examples as her support. Also, ask students what they feel her motive is for including the obscure reference to the Urdu language. Ask the class to discuss whether they feel she is taking other languages as seriously as she is Spanish.

3. Considering Senator Hayakawa s blunt statement, students may find it in agreement with Rovira s commentary on "language rights." However, why do things become so problematic when the term bilingual education is mentioned? Ask students to review Rovira's segue from language rights to bilingual education to see how far Senator Hayakawa would agree and where he would begin to disagree.

4. Lead students in evaluating the article for statements of bilingual education in practice. There are many paragraphs that include appeals to the readers, but only paragraph 15 says something about how a bilingual program constructs its days. Ask students to come up with a list of questions they would like answered about a bilingual program's daily classroom activities. Why do they think Rovira or the other authors in this section have not included such details?

5. In her essay Rovira states "ill-informed politicians and xenophobic voters" as well as "people who don t understand its virtues" killed bilingual education in California. Ask students to examine her essay to see if she makes mention of *who* these people are and *what* their voting reasons were to analyze whether she has supported her accusations. While she acknowledges both sides, students may find after this exercise and after comparing her directly to Garvin that her article is rooted in emotion instead of factual support.

## WHAT'S WRONG WITH BILINGUAL EDUCATION? IS IT "LINGUAL" OR IS IT "EDUCATION"?

1. Ask students to isolate these 3 reports (paragraphs 2-6) and write up descriptive outlines for each. That is, make a statement of what the report *says* and then what the report *does* for the entire essay. This will ask them to read closely to see where these three reports facts are later rehearsed.

2. Defining education policy as what a child should learn in the American school system (proficiency in the English language) and then language policy as the sustaining of one's native language and culture within a school system, students' opinions may vary as to how they feel bilingual education balances such policies.

3. Student answers will vary although it could be wholly agreed upon that this policy showed America to be resistant of other cultures' ability to exercise power within America. In terms of things changing, as the gender stereotypes section proves, while America is still accepting of others, they indeed remain "the other." Nevertheless, such a pronouncement is not likely to be made today for several reasons: the wave of political correctness and the strength with which "immigrant children" now speak and protest.

4. According to Yzaguirre, "white ethnic" Americans are native born children of immigrants. Paragraph 13 offers their viewpoint that all

should learn English because their forefathers were forced to. Using tax dollars to give immigrants back their heritage now via bilingual education goes against the experience their families went through. Ask students to debate this issue.

5. The example of Canada is a problematic one although its main difference from the debates in America about bilingual education is that both pro and con Canadians (to Quebec s separatism) are opposed to bilingual education. Also, there is no chance for a "balkanization" of states from the nation as there is in Canada. Questionable, though, is the idea of "One Canada" or "the promotion of bilingualism in the name of unity." Do students see the same motive in America after reading these four accounts about bilingualism?

6. Yzaguirre's views on this topic are found in paragraph 17. An interesting wrap up to this section could be done as follows: group students by author and have them summarize the claims made by each one on the board. Discuss these evaluations of perspectives and then compare/contrast them.

# CHAPTER ELEVEN
## *FREEDOM OF EXPRESSION*

## CENSORSHIP ON CAMPUS: SHOULD THERE BE LIMITS TO FREE SPEECH?

### REGULATING RACIST SPEECH ON CAMPUS

1. Lawrence comments in the first paragraph that the protection of racist speech from government regulation "reinforces out society's commitment to tolerance as value, and that…we will be forced to combat it as a community." An alternative means of combating racist speech might be public protests and demonstrations.

2. Lawrence establishes himself from the very beginning as someone who questions authority and who ardently defends individual rights. This is further demonstrated by his refusal to participate in a civil defense drill, a school/national activity. His strategy is to set himself up as seemingly inflexible on such issues to underscore the dangerous consequences of unrestricted racist speech which, in the next paragraph, he concedes has strong opposition.

3. Lawrence believes that by framing the issue this way, racial bigots end up morally elevated while fanning "the rising flames of racism." Lawrence says that racist language is an assault on its victim, not an invitation to dialogue. Thus, he feels we should not make the First Amendment one of domination. Also, by allowing unrestricted rights to those who practice hate language, we allow both the psychic injury and racial victimization of minority people to continue.

4. Student answers will vary.

5. Lawrence's argument is based on the principle that the First Amendment does not project utterances that "inflict injury or tend to incite an immediate breach of peace"; racist speech injures and incites

Direct students to paragraph 5 where Lawrence discusses "fighting words" as an exception to the First Amendment. Other than using the words of the amendment itself, students may find that his argument offers too few specific examples.

6. Open for class discussion and/or presentations.

## THE BETRAYAL OF LIBERTY ON AMERICA'S CAMPUSES

1. Kors uses this article to speak out against the repressive effect of speech codes. His examples in paragraphs 2 and 3 demonstrate that the results of speech code enforcement are often nonsensical. Student answers will vary.

2. Open for discussion but students can be broken into groups to evaluate his tone/style, support and organization.

3. Kors' reaction is that schools that enforce speech codes are restricting almost all opinions. As stated in paragraph 10, he feels these codes sap the courage, authority, and conscience of young adults who should be relishing in liberty. His idea of censorship as manipulation is the "mandatory political enlightenment" that these codes advance.

4. First ask students what they understand about "political correctness" and how they have heard the term used. In what areas is "political correctness" applied in the academic world? What, then, is the "progressive" view? Once these terms are defined students can discuss how they understand either to be mythically fabricated.

## IN PRAISE OF CENSURE

1. Wills sees censorship as the outright refusal to make public any offensive media. Censure, on the other hand, has more to do with boycotting a certain product (or entertainer, etc.) in order to make an active political statement against it, while still allowing others to

decide for themselves whether the particular situation is offensive or not. Wills authorizes censure in this article.

2. Giving both sides of an argument can have both positive and negative effects on the reader. If the author seems to be sympathetic to the opposition, readers might feel that he or she is confused on the issue and not authoritative enough. On the other hand, presenting both sides makes the author seem well-informed about the topic and, therefore, more credible. Since Wills is calling for censure so that people can make up their own minds, presenting both sides seems to be excellent rhetorical strategy.

3. Since Wills presents some of the pros and cons of the censorship debate in the first paragraph without stating his opinion directly, the reader is drawn into the argument, if only to find out where the author stands.

4. Wills does not agree with her decision. He asserts that she was indeed protecting her institution so that it may benefit from NEA grants in the future. Student opinions on this matter will vary, and class time can also be used to debate the business perspective against the artistic.

5. This essay presents a fairly difficult concept. Thus, the repetition in the conclusion serves to reiterate his point, rather than obscure it. Again, censure asks people to take an active role in the shaping of media and culture. By representing opposing slants, Wills emphasizes the power of the individual to control the media.

6. Apply student answers to this question to form a debate activity. Groups can present Kors' and Wills' views then compare and contrast them. Lawrence's views can be added at the end of the discussion. Try to achieve a consensus regarding views on censorship since all three do agree that restrictions such as censorship and speech codes repress individuals' freedom to express their opinions.

# CENSORSHIP ON THE INTERNET: DOES THIS NEW MEDIUM CALL FOR NEW RULES?

## THE INTERNET: A CLEAR AND PRESENT DANGER?

1. Cleaver's use of the Dave Barry quote sets up her argument that children do indeed have highly advanced computer skills. This also alludes to her points throughout that parents are less computer savvy than are their children, thus necessitating changes regarding the accessibility of pornography on the Internet.

2. Open for discussion. Students can discuss instances when they have searched for subjects (non-pornographic) on the Internet only to discover sites *unrelated* to their topic. Discuss why this happens.

3. Because school systems are still debating over what sex education programs should address, children/teens usually replace spoken information with the visuals offered by media and popular culture as representations of sexuality. The Internet is simply another, if not easier, medium to contact; thus, Cleaver's fear here seems valid. However, students can argue for and against this issue.

4. Open for discussion. Students, to support their own opinions, could do some quick outside research and bring in current newspaper and magazine articles to supplement the discussion of the legal ramifications of this issue.

5. The class can debate this issue guided by the following questions: How much does age matter to viewing pornographic materials? Although children are more computer literate, do they deserve free reign over the computer?

# PROTECTING OUR CHILDREN FROM INTERNET SMUT: MORAL DUTY OR MORAL PANIC?

1. Lead discussion of data accuracy and validity. Since this misrepresented data was still accepted to enforce legislation, students will likely see the weaknesses in the debate for such Internet legislation. The government should not endorse inaccurate data, yet it is problematic that there are significant amounts of pornographic images available. Students may discuss the reasons why the compilers of this data skewed the information, and if their reasons were good, does it in any way justify their presentation of this data?

2. Although Wilkins' views on the Grassley Bill seem neutral, her use of the word "stream" to discuss subsequent legislation comes off as positioning against such laws, especially since it is based on inaccurate research. She might agree with the bill's goal, but the general feeling seems to be that that things have gotten out of hand, as evidenced in her discussion on media exaggeration.

3. Have students review paragraphs 9-13 and make lists of pros and cons of the CDA. Based on what these opinions are and the explicit goal of the CDA, they can then rate ways in which it could or could not affect society.

4. Students can easily compare this view to the debates about children's access to pornography on television as well as phone sex lines. If these problems arise with both the telephone and television already placed in "well-traveled spaces," how could this solution work differently for a computer?

5. Students can look for current reports on the V-chip's effectiveness for television. If it has been working for television, could it also work for computers where new pornographic Internet sites are added everyday? Students could also ponder over *whose* First Amendment rights are in question here. Returning to Cleaver's article, they can extend the

discussion over whether children are to be even included in this debate. You may also wish to address the international nature of the Internet.

6. Rehearse students' thoughts from question 1 on the need for accurate data to make a sound argument. If Wilkins is telling "the truth," do we believe/agree with her more or have we now become generally skeptical of all data?

WHAT PART OF 'NO LAW' DON'T YOU UNDERSTAND?

1. Student answers will vary but an interesting collaborative exercise would be to separate students into groups representing different forms of the media, radio, television, digital world etc. What are the standards of each and which are universal?

2. Although Turner does not discuss very much the idea of parental control, ask students to imagine these two authors in a conversation with one another. What information would each author want to hear more about concerning parental control? If students disagree with their perspectives, can they imagine a *combination* of parental and governmental control?

3. The role of a system operator is the only parental-like figure available on the Internet. As students may already know, many mailing lists and rooms have "list moms or dads" who monitor what information is published with the intention of limiting the discussion to the chosen topic (so not to clutter up mail boxes, etc.). Whether the system operator should be wholly responsible for topic content is up for discussion. Is such responsibility even possible for a 24-hour medium, and does this mean that the system operator controls the dialogue?

4. Review these statements and note their sarcastic tone. Since Bill Gates is the most recognizable and powerful personality in the computer industry, these authors have probably dropped his name since their articles concern the controlling of content on the information

superhighway. Furthermore, Gates is often referred to as controlling the Internet itself via his Microsoft Internet Explorer software standard on every Windows system. If Gates controls the device we use to view the Internet world, how does this fact apply to issues of censorship? Or does it?

5. Throughout his article Turner refers to "established," "bedrock," and "old tried and true" principles. As a lawyer he naturally feels the need to call upon precedent for solutions. Ask students if they make decisions in a manner that refers to precedent. Then discuss what they believe are the First Amendment's principles to gauge whether they refer to it on this issue.

## CENSORSHIP OF BOOKS

THE FREEDOM TO READ

1. This conference statement can be considered a lengthy motivational appeal against bans or warnings on books. While there are no examples offered of specific books in question, it is a conference statement, so its audience is probably familiar with the books considered in need of warnings. Ask students to consider these two sides when judging the ALA's evidence.

2. Have students discuss the social crises America is currently experiencing. Is everyone affected by these? The ALA seems to think that an already tense democracy will become an enraged one if kept from books and voicing their opinions on books, but opponents might be quick to point out that various groups living in our democracy might not consider themselves in a socially tense situation.

3. Break the class up into several groups and present explanations and opinions on each "declaration." Once all are up on the board, ask them to look for places of overlap between the similarities and/or differences.

4. Paragraphs 1 and 9 explain the ALA's perspective on the First Amendment, and students now can compare it to Turner's "lesson" on the First Amendment. Considering the two explanations together, students are likely to have a greater understanding of it; however, isolating the ALA's statements may cause students to see that the ALA is not as comprehensive in its interpretation as Turner is and will judge effectiveness that way.

5. Student answers will vary.

6. Paragraph 15 addresses the issue of book labeling. In sum, they are against others (publishers and editors) thinking for their readers/customers. Ask students if and how they differentiate a label from a warning. Discussion could continue of students have recently seen books with labels and/or warnings. What do they think would constitute a questionable book these days?

BANNED BOOKS WEEK 1997: A CASE OF MISREPRESENTATION

1. McKinzie's statement could be considered a use of slanted language to draw his reader into the separate sides of the issue. Lead students in a discussion of its effectiveness, particularly at the beginning of his essay.

2. After reviewing their definitions of censorship from the preceding articles in this chapter, students may find that McKinzie's remarks in paragraph 7 illustrate a blurred line between challenges to books and the advocating of censorship.

3. The purpose of the Banned Book List is offered in the first paragraph. McKinzie is trying to prove that the ALA is misguidedly bringing up a dead issue.

4. Since we have been given a statement from the ALA, students could try to imitate its language and structure to reply to McKinzie's statement.

5. Would renaming the event silence McKinzie or is he against the ALA's opinions altogether? Return to student answers from question 3 and extend the discussion. The fact that he is a librarian is persuasive because it proves that although they may have the same overarching goals, librarians too question authority and challenge the ALA. Do students consider him a "dissenter" like Charles Lawrence considered himself?

## AUTHOR'S AFTERWORD FROM FAHRENHEIT 451

1. Have students locate examples of Bradbury's word choice that suggest one or all of these tones and then share how *they* as an audience received them. Bradbury's message here is that he is a writer and an artist, who will continue to write his stories the way he wants to and not the way people suggest he write them. His tones suggest he has no patience for interference.

2. Paragraphs 10, 16 and 24 all include what Bradbury infers would be "acceptable," and these descriptions are all negative. For instance, an acceptable book would be "reduced to nursery rhymes" or, more pointedly, be a "nonbook."

3. Students with knowledge of the subject matter of Fahrenheit 451 will recognize the allusion. Basically, he is saying that censorship can take on a variety of forms (as all of the readings in this chapter have shown). Have students make up a list of forms censorship can take, i.e., editing, refusal of publication, revisions, placement on a banned list, etc.

4. Job is a character from the Bible who was a just man tested by God without understanding why. Bradbury, too, is implying that he is an

upright man/author, tested by the general population. Job felt that he didn't deserve to be tested, because he was doing all that a just man should do. Yet he was punished without provocation. Bradbury feels he is also tested without provocation. Furthermore, he makes an open allusion to the Bible in this Afterword, something some editors wanted to strike out from his texts.

5. Bradbury's life as an author has been troubled by censorship and minority reactions. The only way he can handle such censors is by himself, as a writer writing what he wants and writing against such acts. He will not be bullied into political correctness in order to please the status quo.

# CHAPTER TWELVE
## *MEDIA INFLUENCE*

## ADVERTISING: HOW POWERFUL IS THE LANGUAGE OF PERSUASION?

### WITH THESE WORDS I CAN SELL YOU ANYTHING

1. Most copywriters would not agree with Lutz's contention that advertisements are written to trick the customers. Although they may admit to tapping into popular consciousness it is likely that most would instead argue that the words used in the ads are those that most people are familiar with and respond to positively. The connotations of these words are universally understood, according to those who write the copy for the ads.

2. A product is considered new for a period of six months during a national advertising campaign, and for as long as two years if a product is being advertised in a limited test market. A product is also considered new if it has undergone "a material functional change." This does not have to be an actual improvement in the product; just a simple alteration will qualify it. Thus, it is easy to side-step the regulatory intention by creating a "new" product by adding lemon scent, for instance. In other words, product performance does not have to be improved. These regulations seem to assist efforts of advertisers to mislead the consumer. Consumers should identify exactly what is "new" before buying a product.

3. Student answers will vary.

4. The author uses an informal, chatty, humorous tone throughout the article. Many comments are not only informative and instructive, but quite entertaining. See the ends of paragraphs 18 and 19, for example. He engages the reader very directly in the process of analyzing weasel

words, giving his reader instructions if not commands in order to get them involved

5.  Some readers would prefer that the essay ended at paragraph 50. The parody seems an odd and awkward tack-on. First the theme of the poem, "the power of advertising to meet our needs and solve our problems," is not directly relevant to the preceding discussion of weasel words. Although humorous, why end with a poem about advertising in general when the essay deals with a very specific subject—weasel words? In straining to be funny and entertaining, students may feel that Lutz made a poor choice for a conclusion.

6.  If a manufacturer makes up a trade name for its product, then advertises that only this particular manufacturer has the product, the technique could be considered circular reasoning. For instance, the Goodyear ad, "If it doesn't say Goodyear, it can't be polyglas," is really saying, "If it doesn't say Goodyear, it can't be Goodyear's (polyglas) fiberglass-reinforced tire."

## THE LANGUAGE OF ADVERTISING

1.  Open for discussion. Many students will recall the efforts of many groups to have the Joe Camel banned. Students can debate over whether outlawing is an effective solution.

2.  O'Neill says that writers "must glamorize the superficial differences" when product differences do not exist, or they must create differences by getting the audience involved in the action in the ad, not the product itself. Ask students to share examples of current glamorized advertisements that involve the audience.

3.  O'Neill cites seven charges that have been made against advertising. In support of advertising, O'Neill's primary argument is simply that advertising language is only a reflection of the society around it, and that "slaying the messenger would not alter the fact—if it is a fact—

that 'America will be the death of English.'" Furthermore, he says that advertising does not *force* us to buy anything, but rather stimulates the development of new products in the marketplace and conveys certain information. Anticipating the objections lends support to his claims since his rebuttals are logical; students may even note that these are already mainstream beliefs.

4. Any number of symbols may be suggested. O'Neill refers to the use of the color red in the depiction of autumn and fire to suggest warmth, experience, and wisdom. Other symbols could include the strong-armed man on the Mr. Clean detergent bottle. O'Neill believes repeated exposure of such symbols acquire the power to call up in the consumer's mind a host of ideas and images that could not be communicated as effectively in any other way.

5. O'Neill's style could be described as "advertising" style. In his own writing, he makes use of some of the techniques he describes. First, he personalized his writing, involving the reader in the communication process. Several times in the introduction he addresses the reader as *you*. To emphasize his point about the simplicity of language, he supports his narrative with the most effective kind of testimonial available, an invitation for the reader to conduct fog index calculations on ads. Furthermore, O'Neill's own language is simple and direct. In a sense, he is selling the language of advertising in his discussion, without raising his vocabulary or voice. Finally, he carefully engineers his own language to mirror the practices of ad writers by carefully selecting the words.

6. Student answers will vary.

THE SELLING OF REBELLION

1. & 2. Since these questions are closely related, begin by referring to paragraph 7 with its description of the relationship between rebellion and American society. Student opinions will vary as to whether the

connection Leo makes is a valid one, but discussion will likely address the notion that America was founded upon such ideals of rebellion. Historically, America has espoused ideals of freedom and, to a certain extent, rebellion. Ask students to make a list of historical events that they could say are based on the rebellious sprit of an individual or group.

3. Again, baby-boomers date back to the 1950s and 1960s, so the previous discussion could be extended to when this particular group of American society was raised. In evaluating who advertisers target and what desires they target, ask students to review the products mentioned in paragraphs 4-6 and/or to bring in their own examples to determine whether such a connection between the theme of breaking rules and this generation exists. While it may be the case with cars, what about perfumes, etc.?

4. Define modernism and postmodernism for students so that they can have a basic understanding of the chaotic tendencies of postmodernism, e.g., that one does not refer to a single meta-narrative, therefore, there is a continual questioning of authority and no supreme rules to break. Students will likely agree that pop culture and the "anything goes" or "everything is shown" media ignite the flame under such relativistic behavior in advertisements.

5. Open for discussion but remind students of Leo's opening statement that television advertisements like the one for Isuzu are "some of the worst cultural propaganda." Could exposure to such advertisements lead to dangerous behavior with products that promote breaking rules?

# SAMPLE ADVERTISEMENTS

## *Got Milk?*

1. Milk has established certain cues that transcend the slogans used in its changing campaign. Students may recall the phrase "Milk, it does a body good," that preceded the current campaign. The milk moustache has become a common thread running throughout the ads. It is likely that even without a slogan, viewers would recognize advertisements for Milk. Have students discuss how visual cues help sell a product even before they read the slogan.

2. The caption plays upon information the audience probably already knows about the popular TV program "Fraser." The relationships and personalities between the characters from the TV show are reinforced by the ad.

3. Again, the advertisement taps into what the audience probably already knows about the characters from "Fraser." Dr. Fraser Crane and his brother Niles, are portrayed on the program as stiff, proper, cultured characters. Thus, their drinking milk from a wineglass plays upon this characterization. The same is true for the other actors in the advertisement.

4. Before the Milk campaign, milk was considered by many to be largely a beverage for children. The increase in milk sales attests to the success of this campaign and the changing image of milk. Ask students for their opinions on their perception of the product. Do they think the ads have changed the public's perception? How?

5. The old saying "if ain't broke, don't fix it," may apply here. Milk's campaign to increase and improve product recognition and sales has been very successful. Keeping the same basic style of advertising allows Milk to continue to ride this wave of success. Ask students to

evaluate the older slogans such as "Milk, it does a body good," "Milk." and "Got Milk?" Which do they think is better and why?

6. Student answers will vary.

7. The target audience is the age group most familiar with the TV program: individuals between 25-35. A child would probably miss the humor of the ad, but would respond to the image of adults drinking milk. Ask students for their opinions on how each age group would react to the ad and why.

8. The television commercials for the Milk campaign feature an individual who runs out of the product in some way, with desperate consequences. Commercials include a woman who runs out of milk with a household of cats (which presumably rebel); a young college student participating in a isolation experiment who discovers to his horror that he has boxes of cereal but no milk; a box of animal crackers who design to knock over a little girl's glass of milk and thus ensure their survival; and a male carnival goer who puts his milk carton down in a hall of mirrors only to bump into these mirrors as he lunges from side to side, mouth full of dry cookie. The TV ads use the same slogan, however. Students may discuss the reasons for the different marketing techniques between print and electronic media. Teachers may direct students to the http://www.gotmilk.com/ website to research more information.

### Count on Shell

1. The ad features a woman, alone, driving at night with the glare of headlights behind her. A pervading sense of menace is relayed to the audience. It is supposed to alarm the viewer and engage them in the drama that is "unfolding" on the page. This woman is in trouble, and Shell will help her get out of it. The sense of danger would be probably lost if the scene was set in the daytime or the subject featured

a man. Shell is trying to promote itself as the selfless knight in shining armor.

2.  This advertisement probably works equally well with women as with men. Women appreciate the advice and concern Shell offers, while men relate to the socially constructed urge to protect. Students can discuss what gender roles are at work in the advertisement. Does Shell seem "male"? If so, why?

3.  Without the Shell symbol, it might be difficult for the reader to associate the ad with the product. Because gasoline sales themselves rely heavily on symbol recognition—drivers may only have a second to decide which gasoline station they want to go to—associating the symbol with the helpful advice is effective here. Direct students to a discussion on symbol recognition in our culture. What other marketing symbols do we respond to instantly while driving (such as fast food restaurants, hotel signs, etc.)?

4.  For years, gasoline advertising has proved a bit problematic for marketers. Consumers often decide where to buy their gas based on name recognition and the pennies saved per gallon. Therefore, a new marketing technique such as the one Shell uses here is needed. Consumers remember the ad, associate the Shell symbol with helpfulness and protection, and may chose the product over ones that do not resurrect similar feelings.

5.  The woman's expression relays concern, but she is still in control. The impression conveyed is that if she makes the right decisions, based on Shell's advice, she will come out of this dangerous situation unscathed. A less dramatic photograph would probably fail to engage the reader long enough to read the rest of the advertisement. Discuss the way advertisers manipulate consumer emotions to sell products.

6.  Student answers will vary.

## *Laughter Is a Great Workout*

1.  Student answers may vary. Direct students to a discussion on why we stop to read ads and why we turn the page or lose interest.

2.  Unlike many other Coca-Cola advertisements, this ad does not feature the product. Ask students for their opinion on whether this detracts from the effectiveness of the promotion of the product.

3.  This advertisement is for a youthful "20-something" audience. However, teenagers who wish to identify with this age group may also react positively to the ad. Have students analyze the values that are conveyed through the ad–how do clothing, grooming, hairstyle, etc. all contribute to audience identification?

4.  The people featured in the photograph are clearly relaxing and enjoying themselves. The slogan reinforces Coke's playful approach. Readers associate the product with friends, laughter and enjoyment.

5.  The ad gives the viewer the impression that they have caught these people at a particularly happy moment in which they are all enjoying a joke and each other's company. We are spectators of the scene. One implication could be that if we use the product, we too could be part of such a happy scene. If the subjects were looking out of the photo, the ad would lose its detached quality, and would force viewers to become connected to the people in the photo, rather than imagining themselves in the scene.

6.  Student answers will vary.

7.  Many diet soft-drink ads 20 years ago featured only women, frequently in bathing suits. People associated diet sodas with dieting – such drinks were substitutes out of necessity, not choice. This ad not only features men, but all of the people in the photo are casually dressed,

physically fit, and do not seem associate the drink with dieting. Drinking this cola is a desirable choice, not a sacrifice.

## TV NEWS: DO WE FIND IT CREDIBLE?

TV NEWS: ALL THE WORLD IN PICTURES

1. Postman and Powers' opening paragraphs discuss how viewers are vulnerable to misinformation and become defenseless when watching recreations in the news. Paragraph 16 is a good reference as it states how the news is fragmented and can only provide small portions of information. While little is explained in depth, viewers accept the information in this format. Ask students if they have ever disagreed with the news they watched. Their remarks may support the ideas of Postman and Powers in that misinformation can perpetuate whether accurate or not if presented in a familiar and authoritative way.

2. Along with analyzing this statement ask students to parallel it with the statement, "seeing is believing." Students can compare pictures to examples as evidence in arguments.

3. Student answers will vary, but most will find that these "pictures" do offer a context that is only lacking the specifics a news anchor can voice over, i.e., the when and where these events occurred.

4. Open for discussion.

5. As in question 1, students can discuss exceptions to this style of presentation. What kind of news report might they prefer? Does it matter if the news program is offering local or international news?

6. Student answers will vary.

7. Student's opinions may differ with this assessment because it seems to infer that heedless viewers will never understand or "get" the news. What mental preparation would be needed? Can't a viewer make his/her own meaning and coherence of the moving pictures? The irony of course is that one turns to the news for meaning. Students can debate over whether the news is or is not "a kind of rousing light show."

## WATCHING THE EYEWITNESS NEWS

1. Rapping's problems with the local news are that it offers brainless information and lacks a multiplicity of perspectives. In paragraph 5, she states that "The Jeffersonian notion that public media should cover what citizens 'need to know' was not a big consideration. Nor was it a concern to respect the audience's intelligence or diversity."

2. Paragraph 9 offers a projection of what Rapping feels the local news is like everywhere. If this is the form, then the function would only be to offer insight to the particular location. Can students see why the format is the same? They could argue for and against this format while also addressing Rapping's claims that all local news is nothing more than insignificant community gossip.

3. Paragraphs 17 and 18 discuss the idea of "safe" news, which can contrast the "hard" news described in paragraph 12. Rapping's idea is that locals prefer to hear good news rather than bad so that their lives and neighborhoods won't be disrupted. Since her view can be thought of as a universal one—no one wants to be bombarded with bad news— students will likely see logic in her perspective. We want to believe the trouble is always elsewhere.

4. Her tone throughout, again as evidenced by her choice of adjectives, is that of a bitter journalist. Students can also isolate paragraph 15 as a place where her logic breaks down. She states that the local news teams' ways of presenting such community responses is deliberately

demeaning, yet her own claims demean the entire industry of the local news.

5. Student answers will vary and this can be a collaborative class exercise. For the most part, it seems Rapping wants to reduce the amount of time given to weather and sports and other gossipy community news. She would likely prefer that news anchors offer more intellectual commentary on the "local issues of serious import."

## WHY THOSE HIDDEN CAMERAS HURT JOURNALISM

1. Open to discussion. Have students recall other programs where they have seen hidden cameras in practice. What were these reports about? An interesting counterpoint to argue is that although Starobin claims using hidden cameras is "trickery and deception," a repulsive crime was committed at Food Lion. Do students feel that they needed to see the crime or just hear about it?

2. Open to discussion and as the "As you read" prompt suggests, compare Bly's actions to the current examples in Starobin's article.

3. To discuss the appeal of hidden cameras students may return to Postman and Powers' points about a viewer's preference of "moving pictures" and extend that discussion. Ask students to discuss if an interview would have the same impact on the audience as "catching someone in the act."

4. Student answers will vary.

5. The differences lie in the fact that this was a *recreation* of an everyday crime. The other stories were discoveries of crimes using visual support to report the crime. Starobin feels that it is unethical to obtain such evidence by deception. Have students compare the effects of both to determine whether such reporting serves the public interest.

6. Students should first discuss the responsibilities they feel producers *should* have and maintain. Then they can pit these viewpoints against Starobin's claims about how to obtain effective and credible news reports.

## MOVIE AND TV VIOLENCE: HOW DOES IT AFFECT US?

HONEY, I WARPED THE KIDS

1. Cannon cites an impressive array of studies that seem irrefutably to prove an association between media violence and aggressive behavior. Have students examine paragraphs 22 and 23 as they include persuasive claims. Cannon's listing of "highlights from the history of TV violence research" in paragraphs 25-36 also suggests a wealth of scientific research supporting the link.

2. According to Cannon in paragraph 48, programming has in fact changed very little. The arguments of network executives in their own defense have changed, however. Ask students to compare the information in paragraph 18 with that in paragraph 51. In addition, Cannon has found a standard contemporary media response in the words of Steve Allen in *Grand Canyon*: "My movies reflect what's going on; they don't make what's going on" (paragraph 8).

3. Although Cannon effectively proves the link between televised and real violence, students may find his solution both obliquely stated and, to the extent, it is identifiable, problematic. Cannon never directly suggests what action he endorses. Clearly, he is pessimistic about Hollywood's ability to police itself voluntarily, a sense conveyed not only by his article-long derision of the entertainment industry, but also by his account of Senator Paul Simon's ultimately ineffectual attempts to work with the industry on this issue (paragraphs 60-66). By returning to the earlier cited *Grand Canyon* scene to end the essay, though, he clearly expresses skepticism about the degree of industry commitment to this project.

4. Students can discuss the relative value of the scientific studies, which mostly appeal to reason, and the more emotional appeal of the anecdotes, which describe individual tragedies allegedly linked to media violence. Encourage students to notice a somewhat startling problem with Cannon's anecdotal evidence: though his major argument is about televised violence, all of the anecdotal evidence concerns movies. Since film and television raise different issues in terms of regulation, Cannon's failure to draw distinctions between the two could be seen as a weakness in his argument.

5. Cannon compares Hollywood liberals to the NRA in an attempt to discredit the former's laissez-faire attitude toward violence in the media. With this analogy, as with the opening description of the political activities of certain Hollywood stars, Cannon suggests the hypocrisy of the entertainment industry, which is willing to speak to "noble causes far removed from their lives" (paragraph 2) but abandons progressive political positions when their own economic or artistic welfare is at stake. Students can debate over whether the comparison is apt: is the question of the relationship between fiction and reality the same as the question of the relationship between hardware (guns) and reality?

6. Students will notice that the original article appeared in *Mother Jones*, a left-wing publication that prides itself on political activism. Such an audience may be expected to despise both the NRA and any infringements on freedom of speech. Cannon's tendency to press only lightly on the problem of censorship may well indicate an awareness of this audience.

VIOLENCE IS US

1. Scheer supports this claim by pointing out the rating appeal of both fictionalized and real violence. As "endless focus groups conducted by news organizations report," news is watched most often "when death and destruction are at hand" (paragraph 10). Unlike Cannon, Scheer's

argument is that media violence and real violence are mutually dependent. We are drawn to real life violence, which perhaps spawns the popularity of fictionalized violence, which in turn leads to higher crime rates. This circularity is noted in paragraph 8.

2. Scheer is an active opponent of censorship, an attitude students will have already noticed in his reference to "pro-censorship prudes" (paragraph 6). Scheer clearly believes film and television producers need the freedom to tell the truth about how "crime is out of control" (paragraph 11), and that adults need the freedom to "watch what they want" (paragraph 12). He does not feel that children's programming needs to be controlled because censorship simply doesn't work. Students could quickly outline Scheer's and Cannon's remarks on censorship to determine their accuracy and then discuss how the two might react to one another. Students should note that Scheer's treatment of the issue of censorship, even if they do not agree with it, is much more thoughtful and complex than Cannon's.

3. Scheer finds two things troubling about the *Beavis and Butthead* anecdote: first, why parents in a "conservative white upper-middle class community" allowed their children to watch this show; and second—and more importantly—why "children of paradise," recipients of all the privileges America has to offer, find so much "delight in this and other stupidities" (paragraph 16). The question of the show's appeal remains for Scheer a troubling symptom of something wrong with American culture. Students who may themselves have been fans of *Beavis and Butthead*, as well as other "cartoons for mature audiences" like *South Park*, may have a different take on its appeal.

4. Scheer believes that the government should not interfere and that responsibility lies with the parents. He encourages his readers to exercise constitutional liberties in their own homes. In language evocative of the central mechanism of democracy, Scheer suggests the correct response to an offensive program is to "vote—by just turning

the damn thing off" (paragraph 29). Ask students to pit Cannon and Scheer against each other in a class debate to gauge their own opinions over the effectiveness or ineffectiveness of these authors' proposed solutions.

5. Norman Lear is a particularly appropriate spokesperson for the position that television violence results from the imperatives of the bottom line. Lear himself has created "thoughtful prime-time programming." He has credibility as a serious, responsible producer who clearly feels he swims against the tide in his profession. Without endorsing exploitative programming, Lear acknowledges that the prime reason for its existence is advertisers who "know from experience that something hard and outrageous will sell faster than something soft" (paragraph 22).

6. Scheer uses Wayne LaPierre, NRA spokesperson, to highlight a dichotomy between the high moral tone of some news programs and the gratuitous violence of entertainment programming. Scheer endorses LaPierre's claim that the networks are hypocritical when they lecture the NRA on the nightly news "and then...go to their entertainment programming and show all kinds of gratuitous violence" (paragraph 9). Students may notice that Cannon mentions the NRA as a way to indicate the hypocrisy of liberal-leaning media executives.

IN PRAISE OF GORE

1. This theory provides the philosophical underpinnings for Klavan's political point. He refers to Plato and "latter-day Platos" to make his point that the role of the artist is to represent precisely those things that are not a part of our daily lives. These references also prove that the dispute over censorship has its roots in western civilization. And while Klavan concedes that there is some relationship between reality and fiction, he argues that it is "so complex, so resonant, that it is impossible to isolate one from the other, in terms of cause and effect" (paragraph 16).

2. Klavan admits that it may be true that fictional violence allows a harmless outlet for our violent tendencies. But although he finds the cathartic defense reasonable, he is not interested in defending violence; he wants instead to celebrate it. The theory of catharsis is defined in paragraph 25 and students' reactions to ideas regarding the "joy" of violence will vary.

3. Breaking up the argument into sections may help students grasp the overall shape of this relatively long and complex essay. This exercise is an excellent opportunity for small group work and then subsequent class collaboration.

4. Whereas Scheer asks his readers to "face" the inherently unpleasant fact that "we like violence," Klavan's strategy is not to defend the appeal of violence in fiction but to celebrate it. Repeatedly in this essay Klavan refuses the temptation to simply defend the right to produce violent fiction. Students can discuss which approach they find most palatable.

5. On one hand, as a professional writer, Klavan's voice is important in the debate over fictional violence. And partly because he brings a writer's sensibility, Klavan is able to cogitate about philosophical and aesthetic issues as well as social and legal ones. Students who are more critical of Klavan could argue that because he makes his living as a writer of horror literature, he is inherently biased since he stands to suffer financially, as well as artistically, from censorship.

6. Klavan's essay begins with a good defense. The first paragraph is designed to shock. Here, Klavan lists the horrific things he loves. Only at the start of the second paragraph does Klavan tell us he loves these things "only in stories." The opening of the essay dramatically enacts Klavan's determination not to apologize for fictional violence, but, as said before, to celebrate it. Students can dispute whether they found this approach refreshing or offensive.

# CHAPTER THIRTEEN
## *INDIVIDUAL RIGHTS*

## PHYSICIAN-ASSISTED SUICIDE: WHO HAS THE RIGHT TO CHOOSE?

### THE SUPREME COURT AND PHYSICIAN-ASSISTED SUICIDE

1. Angell makes the comparison to Roe v. Wade because assisted suicide is a nationwide debate that terminally ill patients be allowed the right to choose to live or die. Abortion and assisted suicide are similar in that both involve the individual choice of taking a human life. They differ in that the life taken in one instance is a person enduring a terminally ill disease and the other is an unborn life without conscious choice. Students can discuss the similarities and differences they see between the two. Angell may have made this connection because the legality of the choice involved is similar. The patient/pregnant woman is making a decision not to prolong a life.

2. Paragraphs 6 and 7 differentiate the active and passive roles of doctors and patients in assisted suicide and euthanasia. Making a distinction is important because of the moral ambiguity that surrounds the decisions/actions of both. For both the goal is to end suffering, but as she reminds readers euthanasia can be performed without the patient's knowledge and participation. Assisted suicide requires the patient's knowledge and participation.

3. The abuses feared are as follows: Assisted suicide would be a threat to the economically and socially vulnerable. The poor, disabled, and elderly might be coerced to request it. Overburdened families or cost conscious doctors might pressure vulnerable patients to request suicide. Angell's statement that "no human endeavor is immune to abuses" is one to consider as satisfactory, especially since the Roe v. Wade decision did not have such an abusive outcome.

4. Angell uses her story about her father to make an abstract issue concrete, although students could argue that *any* example could have done this. Students can discuss whether or not Angell is credible as a writer when saying, "I have no doubt my father would have chosen [physician-assisted suicide]." Could she know this for certain?

5. Students can argue Angell's statement, "If there is to be assisted suicide, doctors must not be involved." How is this possible? Although we can recognize Angell's points that it is the patient's decision and the patient should not be denied the opportunity to end "unbearable suffering," doctors, according to the Hippocratic Oath, should still play an active role in their patient's care. Students can debate over how much decision-making involvement they would want doctors to have.

## DEATH AND DIGNITY—A CASE OF INDIVIDUALIZED DECISION MAKING

1. Student answers will vary.

2. Both Diane and Tim are diagnosed with leukemia and given a 25 percent chance of survival. The immediate reactions are the same but their ultimate decisions about treatment differ. Diane asks for the Hemlock Society's "recipe" two weeks after her initial diagnosis. While it seems both doctor-patient relationships were familiar ones and based on honesty, Diane and Quill were quicker to come to an understanding about her future life with the disease. As paragraph 6 of the Hendlin article suggests, he and Tim took longer to discuss things in an open manner.

3. Open to discussion. Neither Quill nor Angell give readers the details of where and who would be with the patient during the final moments of an in-hospital physician-assisted suicide. It seems there would be a closer monitoring than Diane's hour alone at home.

4. Quill only indirectly made Diane's suicide possible because he was more of a friend/confidant. While he was sure to offer medical advice, he allowed her all the decision-making power. He did not impose his advice on her; as the title of his article suggests, this was a case of *individualized* decision-making. We can gather that Quill is for the legalization of physician-assisted suicide from paragraphs 7 and 14 where he admits he will take any risks for the patients he really knows and cares about.

## SUICIDE, ASSISTED SUICIDE, AND MEDICAL ILLNESS

1. Student answers will vary.

2. The fears and anxieties of terminally ill patients include becoming burdens on their families and anticipated future suffering. The opening paragraph describes Tim's immediate reaction and his request for support in carrying out his suicide. "He was worried about becoming dependent and feared both the symptoms of his disease and the side effects of treatment.

3. As Tim's case suggests, there is often a preceding inability to share feelings or handle depression. Terminally ill patients need to feel wanted and that they are still valuable members of society, not just sick people in need of medical care.

4. Open to discussion. Students can create a list of reasons why doctors need/want to maintain control and compare it to a list of reasons why patients might feel a similar need/want of control. The "real issue" for patients is fear, which needs to be handled by caring physicians appropriately. In essence, frustration cannot take over. Doctors and patients must have an open dialogue.

5. If life is defined as a "pursuit of happiness," it will not change when referring to the terminally ill as long as the patient, like Tim, takes

advantage of his remaining days to be honest and open with family and friends. Hendlin's use of this quote infers the need to do something to give meaning to life, which is applicable to both the healthy and the terminally ill.

## THE RIGHT TO PRIVACY: IS IT BEING VIOLATED?

THE WAR AT HOME

1. Vidal profiles a terrorist as a foreign looking, fez-wearing person who appears too much at ease. What he is really saying is that it is never this easy; one can never tell who is guilty or innocent. Therefore, it is impossible to have a fool-proof machine or system to determine who is a criminal. Vidal's argument is that the government should stop invading everyone's privacy [citizen harassment] with such devices.

2. Vidal comments on the Second Amendment to support his claim that the principles of American government are being abused. This personalized argument seems to suggest he is against its enforcement.

3. Building off of the "As You Read" prompt, have students isolate a few examples of his sarcasm to discuss its influence on his argument. Paragraphs 8 and 9 work to satirize the extreme measures the government is going to supposedly to "protect" its citizens.

4. Advances in technology allow the government to probe more deeply into everyone's lives. Vidal hopes to increase resistance to such government interference. Ask students if they agree with the adage: If more people speak against it, then the government might listen.

5. Vidal's opinion on the war on drugs is that it too has become an invasion of privacy in the form of unlawful attacks and seizures. Again, his sarcasm shines through here in word choice.

6. Vidal believes the real terrorists are the police as evidenced in his concluding paragraph. His assessment is open to discussion. Students may consider the examples Vidal offers as isolated incidents and then conduct some outside research to bring forth further examples of such misguided police behavior.

## PRIVACY FOR SALE: PEDDLING DATA ON THE INTERNET

1. Shapiro's statement implies that privacy defenders feel that there should be a way for surveyors *not* to gain access to personal data. However, such privacy protection should be a purchasable option. Students can debate for and against paying for privacy basing their opinions on the comment that likens the value of information to an asset.

2. One example of the price of privacy is that one might miss out on the market the Internet provides. Ask students to discuss Shapiro's statement "While privacy can conceal scourges from scrutiny, it is more often a fulcrum of democracy presenting other basic freedoms, including rights of association of free speech, voting, and the pursuit of liberty and happiness."

3. Open to discussion.

4. Assign small groups a problem to analyze considering each as an item of support. Is one more effective than another? Shapior's support consists of factual examples and statistics as well as hypothetical situations.

5. International law recognizes privacy as a fundamental human right, and the EU has limited personal data transfer. Americans cling to the belief that America is the protector of *all* freedoms. Europeans, however, do not focus on this issue or harbor such illusions of privacy preservation, which may be why such arguments over privacy in Europe are rare.

6. Shapiro's solution imitates the system in Europe of a minimum level of personal information; privacy that cannot be bartered away. This solution would make personal information privacy the norm, not the exception. Also, data pushers will have to justify their practices. Evaluation of this solution could be constructed as a debate pitting data pushers against Internet customers or innocent searchers.

## IMPERIAL BEDROOM

1. Franzen believes privacy is a legal mess because conceptions of personal autonomy are clouded. For example, in paragraph 7, students can discuss Franzen's speculation that individuals are actually more concerned with a feeling of privacy; it is a more emotional than objective issue.

2. PrivacyGuard says "it will put you in the know..." but shouldn't any and every credit card offer such control over account records? Franzen's story supports his overall argument that when attempting to gain control over privacy, it is often not worth it. Therefore, people should not put themselves in a panic over privacy.

3. To discuss their opinions of what constitutes "good reasons to sacrifice privacy," students can evaluate the examples Franzen mentions in paragraph 12, such as airport X-rays, Megan's Law and drug-testing of student athletes. Review the Shapiro and Vidal essays for their specific claims and compare them to Franzen's belief that too much has been made about the protection of privacy. All of the authors in this section discuss an over-anxiousness that plagues Americans today, but how do students feel about compromising privacy?

4. Student answers will vary. Some of the other values likely to be considered are love, success, education, family, etc.

5. Franzen believes America has fallen victim to a post hoc fallacy that started with the idea that "There is less privacy than there used to be."

He says the claim has been made or implied so often by the media that Americans believe it and express it to others.

6. Open to discussion. Students can itemize one of their days and list how their digital footprints could be traced via receipts, school identification cards, attendance to classes and/or socials, computer log-ons, telephone calls, etc.

## STUDENTS AND DRUG TESTING: OFFENSE OR DEFENSE?

HIGH COURT TAKES ON SCHOOL ATHLETES AND DRUG TESTING

1. Will is against drug testing as evidenced by his tone (see paragraph 6). He is also specifically against schools acting in *loco parentis*.

2. Discuss the trends and platforms of each former President and why each Justice may reflect those priorities as they react to the issue of drug testing.

3. The idea is similar because it comments on how school is a place for education, not interruptions of drug testing, just as the highway is to travel. Other analogies within the section are the examples of witch-hunting and the long-haired men. This parallelism is open for discussion, especially when considering the factor of suspicion.

4. Student answers will vary.

5. Student answers will vary.

TESTING FOR DRUGS, WITCHES, AND LEFTOVER MILK

1. Ask students for their first reactions to this title. While it is an odd commingling of subjects, each of the three words/phrases become examples in the article that all argue over the determinability of testing as a practice.

2. Students will likely agree that junior high and high school students are *not* considered children. By this age in school they are considered adolescents and have adult-like commitments and drive for their chosen sport. Students can argue against this terminology, and discuss its usefulness as a rhetorical strategy. Also, compare the "regulation" of students in schools by teachers with the regulation of student athletes by coaches.

3. The concept of the witch-hunt stems from the practice of a community attempting to identify individuals who they believed practiced witchcraft and so posed a general threat to the well-being of the community. Naturally, many innocent people were accused of this invisible "crime." The term now applies to any fervent persecution of people who are under suspicion, often without any basis, of promoting harm to the populace, such as in the McCarthy communist scare during the 1950s with its blacklisting of actors, musicians, etc. The parallels between witch-hunts and random drug testing relate to the levels of harassment involved and the feeling that it is permissible to sacrifice a few innocents for the concept of greater good. Ask students to identify other parallels between witch hunting and drug testing.

4. Natriello supports his argument by first detailing the legal policy at the root of the controversy, then its negative consequences on the relationships between parent and child and student and teacher. Group work can be done to evaluate his points. Students can share their opinions on how pertinent they feel the level of trust is between the school system and the student and if they feel drug testing is demeaning.

5. Claude Lewis will likely disagree with Natriello and argue that the larger problem is drug use and the presence of drugs in schools. Natriello's focus on emotions and relationships between the student and his parent/coach/teacher is not of serious concern to Lewis.

6. The objective behind drug testing is to deal with the threat of drugs in schools and communities and therefore prevent its spread and long-term use/addiction. Whether student athletes are the right population to target is open to debate. Students can pit Lewis against Natriello—all students vs. student athletes. Within the education system, which group do students feel is the more necessary to test?

## NAÏVE COURT DIDN'T GO FAR ENOUGH WITH DRUG TESTING

1. Open to discussion.

2. Students can debate over whether they consider the youth of today "unsuspecting." The can also evaluate their own high school experience in response to Lewis' reasons for drug testing.

3. This statement contrasts with paragraph 7 which is entirely based on the idea that the drug problem is a universal one—not limited to one community.

4. His tone, which alternates between militant and resigned, creates an emotional appeal. Readers can interpret his feelings on the issue, but whether they agree with him and become supporters of drug testing themselves is up for discussion.

5. It is a sad victory because the Fourth Amendment has been used to limit the rights of *students*, young adults trying to receive an education.

6. Paragraphs 2 and 3 offer the solution to randomly drug test all students, not just student athletes. Drug testing along with education and parental involvement, make up Lewis' solution for preventing future drug users and addicts.

7. Open to discussion. Students will likely point out the lack of evidence in the article and the fact that Lewis relies on blanket statements as in paragraph 12.

# JUST SAY NO TO RANDOM DRUG TESTING

1. Have students speculate reasons as to why the Ridgefield school decided to implement a drug testing policy. Is it, as Rocah says, because they improperly read the 1995 Supreme Court decision? Is it perhaps a "better safe than sorry" mindset? If it is true that the majority of student athletes are law abiding citizens, then it would seem to still depend on suspicion and justifiable concern.

2. According to many legal scholars, yes, Fourth Amendment rights do apply to students under 18 years of age. Break students up into groups to each represent a key player in the lawsuit, remembering that Roach's aim is to increase student's knowledge and respect for the Constitution.

3. As a member of the ACLU, Rocah has been exposed to a variety of civil-rights cases. This authority allows him some ability to project to what people will and will not object, but we can argue that he cannot know for certain what schools would do. Other examples are in paragraphs 11 and 12, where he speaks for other groups without referring to any documented evidence. Students can discuss whether they feel his legal experience is enough to support such opinions.

4. Student answers will vary. To extend the discussion, ask students for opinions about why this is the assumption about student athletes.

5. Students will find these facts only slightly detract from the central issue of random drug testing in schools. They work to Rocah's advantage, though, in that they offer reasons why random drug testing is not necessary and why schools (and parents) need to hone their skills as keepers of order and discipline.

# CHAPTER FOURTEEN
## *REGULATING RELATIONSHIPS*

## SAME SEX MARRIAGES: IS CURRENT SOCIAL POLICY FAIR?

VIRTUALLY NORMAL

1.  The basis of this concern is the conservative view that "homosexual life...is worse than heterosexual life." Sullivan addresses this claim by reminding readers that homosexuals already belong to heterosexual families.  As he points out in paragraph 5, it is the heterosexual familial rejection of homosexuals that destroys families.  Have students discuss which perspective they support and why.

2.  Student answers will vary.

3.  To illustrate Sullivan's use of "they" when speaking of the conservatives, refer to the following statement in paragraph 3: "They mean by all this 'the other,' against which any norm has to be defended and any cohesive society protected."  This terminology persuades the reader to consider the conservatives "the other" instead of homosexuals.  Therefore, something is not right/normal with the way "they" are thinking and arguing against homosexual marriages.

4.  The reasons for homosexual depravity include familial rejection.  By including both views of the issue, Sullivan uses the argument of depravity to prove that the conservative views beg the question.  Students can discuss whether they found this identification of fallacies a strengthening point of his essay.  After examining Sullivan's points they may also try to find fallacies that weaken his own argument.

5.  Hadley Arkes' claim, in sum, is that men need women.  Sullivan uses Arkes' argument to discuss the option of heterosexuals remaining single. If they can remain bachelors, why can't homosexuals; and

conversely, if men need to marry another for care and support, why can't that person be a man? In discussing Sullivan's evaluation of Arkes, direct students to paragraph 8 and the argument about what is "socially preferred," marriage or bachelorhood? Also ask students if they think Arkes was really advocating "feminizing society." The need of a female influence in a man's life is not the same thing as feminizing society.

6. Waverers are single people who waver on the decision of marriage. The only options are to marry or remain single. In terms of gay marriages, conservatives refuse to embrace virtuous homosexual men, but for wavering women, a lesbian relationship is socially preferable. These views are all based on Arkes' argument about the necessary presence of women.

7. Open to discussion. Have students describe the qualities of both audiences. Is one more liberal than another? Or is there a large majority of college students who are equally conservative?

## AGAINST HOMOSEXUAL MARRIAGE

1. The passage from *Leviticus* gives the source of religious opposition. Student's responses to the passage and to Wilson's use of it will vary.

2. Wilson's article is source-heavy and a point by point critique of Sullivan's views. Sullivan's essay leans more towards an acknowledgment of both sides of the debate and less of an attack on conservative views.

3. Natural law is that "man cannot live without the care ad support of other people." It would seem that the all-encompassing "man," as well as the ambiguous "other people," leave this law open to application to homosexual marriages.

4. In evaluating Wilson's argument ask students to consider whether such a statement justifies all types of relationships and their problems. He does not want "tampering with the system" because he feels the legalization of homosexual marriages would parody or "weaken an already strained" institution of marriage.

5. Student answers will vary. Sullivan would likely concede to the truth in this idea since his argument is against the majority conservative view, meaning the liberationists are the minority.

6. Wilson's reference to Sullivan is a clear attack on the author and homosexuals. He believes marriage is a "serious" institution and implies that gays would marry only to parody the status quo. Moreover, he depreciates Sullivan's character as a gay male by implying that Sullivan himself would not marry because gay men, by Wilson's definition, are all promiscuous. Debate this issue and also detail the differences/similarities between promiscuous college males versus homosexual males. Is such behavior more acceptable in one population over another?

FOR BETTER OR WORSE

1. The American definition of marriage relies on emotions and "lifelong love." In Japan, there is a belief that marriage is a partnership or investment in social stability; not as much emotional fulfillment is necessary. Student may feel that Japanese society may be more accepting of homosexual marriages since it does stress social stability. On the other hand, the concept of gays wishing to marry because they are in love may not be understood by Japanese society by these same standards.

2. The Hayekian view is faulty in that non-legal rules are arbitrary; marriage, however, is a legal institution. Rauch, on the other hand, acknowledges that rules do not always reflect the customs of a culture, and may, in fact, deviate from the rules. It would seem logical, then to

admit that laws and legal institutions can and even should change to reflect social norms. The Hayekian view, however, is one of extremes: no more social reforms or laws. Society is unchangeable and unadaptable.

3. Deprivation of heterosexual *and* homosexual marriages are not minor issues. Such thoughts assume all are in favor of marriage as society's most fundamental institution.

4. Some of the issues implied in this quote are biology, procreation, and adoption; homosexual relationships are not the only ones that do not produce children.

5. Open to discussion.

6. As paragraph 30 states, "being tied to a committed relationship plainly helps stabilize gay men." If gays were allowed to marry, the stereotypical "promiscuous gay male" might advance serious relationships more often. Gay marriages might serve the conservative principles that believe in traditional marriages of lifelong stability. Use this question to extend the discussion started in question 1.

7. Wilson might disagree with this essay. While he would concede that it is good for society to have people attached and that marriage is a privileged institution, he would completely disagree with the option of gay marriages as one taken advantage of.

## SEXUAL HARASSMENT: SHOULD WE ESTABLISH RULES OF BEHAVIOR?

EQUAL EMPLOYMENT COMMISSION: TITLE VII GUIDELINES ON SEXUAL HARASSMENT

1. Student answers will vary. Have students share their prior knowledge of the term sexual harassment.

2. Similar to the "As you read" suggestion, allow students to share their opinions over whether the wording is straightforward or ambiguous.

3. Student answers will vary.

4. Student answers will vary.

## THE END OF HARASSMENT

1. In the age of political correctness there is an intensified sensitivity to all minority groups' feelings. The "fashion" is that everyone is oppressed in some way so everyone is asking for special treatment.

2. Open to discussion. Referring to paragraph 9 will help students determine what to include and what is already included in other civil and criminal laws.

3. Dooling wants an amendment passed to return Title VII back to its original intent, but with more specific language. An amendment that specifically prohibits sexual discrimination in terms/conditions of employment. Ideally, this amendment would accomplish uniformity in the treatment of individuals at work and in society.

4. The Paula Jones case is a good example of Dooling's claim that Title VII§1604.11 is being used too often. His opposition might remark that this amendment should not be revised because it has the power to defend individuals from harassment from the most powerful individuals; even Presidents cannot escape depositions. The Kennedy affairs as most of Clinton's were consensual and not harassment. Bringing up Kennedy weakens his argument because it bears little to no relevance.

5. Open to discussion. Ask students if they personally were persuaded to rethink the wording, intentions, or use of Title VII.

6. Students will likely agree that Dooling's final question is an accurate assessment of sexual harassment in the workplace, or between people who work together as the Paula Jones case demonstrates. Offenses that involve physical actions usually do happen "behind closed doors", i.e., when a man and a woman go "into a room together and come out with different stories."

## HETEROPHOBIA: SEXUAL HARASSMENT AND THE FUTURE

1. Ask students to evaluate whether Patai's experiences fit under the description of sexual harassment given in Title VII: "Unwelcome sexual advances, requests for sexual favors, and other verbal or physical conduct of a sexual nature." Some of her examples do fit, but not all happened in work environments. Furthermore, none of them affected the work environment and she was in no real danger.

2. Open to discussion. In discussing the double standard of policies, ask students how they feel about Patai's own experiences and admissions of what has happened to her and then what she admits to having done.

3. Open to discussion. Students will likely agree that these cases are extreme examples and not necessarily the norm. In particular, some of the cases involved behaviors, hugging and offhand remarks, that do not fit under Title VII's definition of sexual harassment.

4. Paragraph 12 discusses "sex regulators" who want to dismantle heterosexuality altogether. However, Patai then switches the focus to feminist reformers. It does not seem that sex regulators *or* feminists would want to ban sex and alienate their public. It is also never clarified if the "hostile environment" and "reasonable woman" standards are based in feminism. Paragraph 16 offers more comments about the feminist perspective which might help students determine their involvement in the stand for/against sexual harassment legislature, but Patai fails to inform her readers of the connection.

5. Paragraphs 10 and 11 detail some of the measures professors have taken to avoid sexual harassment charges. While these are not exactly extreme, students can debate over whether they are necessary.

6. Academic institutions are no longer places where academic theories can be played out and taught. There is no more pursuit of intellectual and personal relationships between teachers and students. Attention to sexual harassment makes campuses "danger zones where abuse lurks in every corner." Discuss the concept of caution detracting from teaching as a natural practice.

SEX IS THE LEAST OF IT: LET'S FOCUS HARASSMENT LAW ON WORK, NOT SEX

1. In paragraph 4 Schultz notes that sexual harassment is more of an issue of sexists' failure to take women seriously as workers. Paragraphs 5 and 6 offer various examples of male mastery and reinforcement of gender indifference.

2. Schultz would likely respond positively to Dooling's commentary as they hold similar views on shifting the focus to the issue of discrimination in the workplace. She might react negatively to him personally, though, because his tone reflects an attitude of women taking advantage of the option of Title VII, i.e., the "parade of women." Dooling's article is more about sexual advances while Schultz centers on gender discrimination.

3. Schultz feels sexism is more dangerous than advances or innuendoes because it takes on the form or work sabotage. Students' own opinions about which is more dangerous will vary.

4. The examples in paragraphs 9 and 10 and their applicability to Title VII can be debated individually. Collectively, they do not meet the standards of Title VII because this amendment is about sexual

favors/conduct. However, they do describe situations that began as sexism then took the form of verbal harassment/misconduct on the job.

5. All of the authors in this section place some of the blame for Title VII's overuse or misuse on feminist groups. Overview the articles for mention of feminists: Patai refers to their latching onto sexual harassment in paragraph 16 and Dooling remarks in paragraph 11 that of late feminists have admitted Title VII is vague. The connection is made between feminism and sexual harassment law since the majority of cases are made against patriarchal attitudes.

6. Paragraph 12 describes the hostility men can feel from other male co-workers. Threats to manliness and manhood are more common than Disclosure's example of a proposition from a female boss.

7. Schultz's overall argument is unique in this group of readings because it makes the argument about Title VII's misinterpretation more direct—much of the time sexual harassment *is* sexism. The idea involved in all of the articles is the incentive to use Title VII to protect workplaces. Students can review the authors' examples to list what type of behaviors need to be excluded from work environments; make sure to differentiate between sexism and sexual harassment.

## ADOPTION: DO SEALED RECORDS VIOLATE OR PROTECT OUR RIGHTS?

ADOPTION AND THE SEALED RECORD SYSTEM

1. Student answers will vary.

2. The two situations are not parallel because parents who give up their children for adoption do so voluntarily knowing what this action imports. "Walking out" is not the appropriate phrase in either case because divorced parents who relinquish custody may do so just to make the transition into a new family structure easier for the child (as

opposed to a custody battle in the courtroom). Furthermore, children adopted at birth have no association with their birth parents while children of divorce often have years.

3. The "mutual consent system" is the releasing of identifying information to birth parents, adoptive parents, and adoptees who have reached the age of 18. Search movement organizations want open records for those (supposed) large numbers of adopted parents and children who want to locate each other. These individuals want more than health, genetic and social information—correspondence and visitation are their goals.

4. Bartholet discusses the search movement's claim that biology is central to parenting in paragraph 10. They use this claim to support reunions of birth parents and children. They feel open communication is needed so not to be left in "genealogical bewilderment." An informational link is needed to preserve biologic families. Students can discuss whether biology truly makes the parent, as Bartholet implies.

5. Students can debate yes or no on this issue. A new birth certificate does seem false, but if parents have relinquished all ties, then in effect the adoptive families will forever be the parents and should be identified as so on a birth certificate.

6. Bartholet's position on adoption is that it should be understood as a positive alternative to biologic parenting and not as a desperate last resort, either for birth parents or the infertile. Her suggested solution is a reversal of the current presumptions about identifying information: open the records and allow the parties to request closure.

7. She bases this assertion on her opinions: "I don't imagine that there would be more than limited communication between adoptees and their birth relatives in most instances. But I may be wrong…" These statements almost make readers question why she even wants open records if not that many adoptees or birth parents will use them.

Bartholet is essentially proposing an idea despite the fact that she has no real knowledge of the actual final outcome.

## STRENGTHENING FAMILIES

1. Open to discussion. Students can detail each concept then collaborate to determine Brosnon's connection.

2. Authority may lie in knowing *and* experiencing the legal issues that surround adoption. Brosnon claims he is not an expert because he is not well versed in the law that surrounds adoption and the open record policy.

3. The myth of the chosen baby is that s/he was the chosen one. Attached to this myth is the concept that the child was specially chosen or picked over all other children, even biological ones. What is faulty with this story is that it is based on deceit, which is not in the child's best interests.

4. Paragraph begins Rev. Brosnon's discussion of loss including the loss felt by those infertile. He also attempts to describe the loss felt by the birth mother and then states that the greatest loss is suffered by the adopted person. He then juxtaposes the loss by/from adoption with relinquishment.

5. The emotion of anger is either suppressed or becomes destructive and violent. Brosnon offers himself as an example of a raged adoptee and compares his emotion to Moses who also welled up his rage. Regarding the issue at hand, sealed adoption records intensify rage over the years.

6. A myriad amount of religious concepts or references are used in this piece. Students' opinions may vary over whether they detract from Brosnon's speech or not. Besides invoking the Catholic Bishops of the U.S.'s Book of Blessings, he uses his example of receiving Holy

Orders as the moment when he overcame illegitimacy. Paragraphs 26 and 27 discuss Dualism versus True religion in terms of integrity. He also feels "The adopted person's search for his origins is a spiritual journey, a pilgrimage of self-knowledge, a holy endeavor." Finally, he calls upon St. Anthony of Padua, patron saint of the barren *and* the pregnant.

## ERASING THE RIGHT TO PRIVACY

1. Both Bartholet and Brosnon advocate open records, but neither addresses the possibility of the open records policy resulting in stalking. Have students re-evaluate their articles to see if this point was alluded to or could be inferred from the type of open records system they advocate.

2. Paragraph 8 discusses how some adopted individuals now have to resort to defensive tactics. The central issue is the desire to pursue contact and how it has occurred thus far.

3. Lurking people could be both birth parents and birth children eager to satisfy their own needs over the comfort and privacy of the other party. Thus, some adopted children and birth parents are reduced to checking over their shoulders fearful that they will be "found" against their wills. This statement supports his overall point that the NCFA is for adoption and respects the privacy of those parent-child relationships.

4. Based on the freedom of information that open records offer, a triad decision is not likely to work. To illustrate, an adoptee might want to exercise his "contact veto" and limit the informational content made public. However, a birth parent might want such information restricted and claim the open records policy allows them access to it.

5. Open to discussion.

# ON THE CONFIDENTIALITY OF ADOPTION RECORDS

1. Comparison of authors can be structured as group presentations. However, Brosnon's personal example, in particular, is a detailed one to reference for the viewpoint of an adopted adult. He also gives his mother's story.

2. Student answers will vary.

3. Open to discussion. The idea of permanence is clarified in paragraph 7: "Adoption creates in the legal and social sense new, permanent families and nullifies all rights, responsibilities and relationships with the family of origin."

4. As in question 1, students can refer to Brosnon's speech and speculate how his mother, who had one child every year, dealt with loss, if at all.

5. The emphasis is placed on medical and social history information, which the NCFA says can be shared without identifying information and without divulging personal information the other parties' pasts. Paragraph 15 agrees with this idea of right to information: "Children who were placed in adoptive homes should not be treated any differently than children born into a family."

6. Paragraphs 26 and 27 discuss the difficulty of the decision birth parents make when they choose between privacy and reform. Students can be broken into groups by author to respond to NCFA's claim and stand on confidentiality and permanence. The NCFA believes it is essential to look beyond the rhetoric of "happy family reunions" to the basic human rights involved in the debate. Not all reunions are sure to be happy ones.

# THE PROMISE OF CONFIDENTIALITY

1. The "we" in Schaefer's article encompasses a variety of groups—birth mothers, unwed mothers, and then a collective "we" in paragraph 8. In sum, she uses it to speak for women who have given a child up for adoption.

2. "Secrecy and lies" was the reality for pregnant young women in Schaefer's day, which persisted even after they gave their children up for adoption. Confidentiality would have allowed these mothers escape from such mistreatment.

3. Student opinions of her assessment will vary. She supports this perspective with 14 years of observations. She states the common fear in being found by birth children is the fear of losing the love of the people currently in their lives. She feels that women should face the fear because the reunion is an "incredible blessing." Students can debate whether all mothers would ultimately feel as Schaefer did.

4. Schaefer's effectiveness is open to discussion.

# CHAPTER FIFTEEN
## CASEBOOK: JUVENILE CRIME, ADULT TIME?

### YOUTH CRIME HAS CHANGED—AND SO MUST THE JUVENILE SYSTEM

1. Students will likely agree that the juvenile justice system is dated. Reilly's opening paragraph gives the most information about the creation of the system, but students could also do some outside research of the 1899 establishment. Paragraphs 6-9 offer suggestions of what should be done to update it, which includes prioritizing public protection instead of relying on the optimistic view that things will improve.

2. Paragraphs 1 and 2 define "parens patriae" as the act of the state becoming the parents of underage criminals. Student answers will vary on its "place" in the criminal justice system.

3. Discussion of this word choice will vary. Students could consider "numbing" to mean indifference or shocking, which is more persuasive to readers of Reilly's argument. Therefore, it is important to differentiate who it is becoming numb, the criminals or the general population? An increase in numbers can almost paralyze us and then cause us to react against such behaviors while criminals who repeat offenses become numb to the actions they commit.

4. Open to discussion and/or debate. Ask students if they can think of criminals who have been rehabilitated. If they can, how is such rehabilitation determined and was it dependent on age?

5. Like question 3, students are asked to pay close attention to language and determine its multiple possibilities. Students should discuss if they noticed this word choice on the first read or only after re-reading. Can they suggest more persuasive language?

6. Direct students to paragraphs 8 and 9 which detail the specific legal responsibilities. Discussion of the pros and cons of these recommendations can revolve around fairness and feasibility.

## ADULT CRIME, ADULT TIME

1. Open for discussion, but direct students to sections such as paragraph 5 for definitions of the two terms. If a delinquent is a neglected or rebellious child whose actions are those of a truant, vandal or petty thief, what constitutes a "criminal"? With regard to the justice system, however, more is made of the difference between children and criminals than of delinquents and criminals.

2. Refer to the history provided in paragraph 8. Compare this information with what students already know. Their thoughts on the juvenile system may stem from the operating principle Collier mentions.

3. Collier does not offer a solution to the shortcomings of *guardian ad litem*. The connection between her explanation of this system and her argument is that it proves juveniles who have not committed serious crimes are not helped by a coddling system; therefore, more criminal justice intervention is needed for those who do commit adult crimes.

4. Megan's law requires that advance notification be given to a neighborhood when a convicted sexual predator re-enters their community. Although it is unclear whether Jesse Timmendequas was a juvenile criminal, the "national outrage" and eventual legislation that was passed proves, and thereby supports, Collier's argument. If people voice their opinions loud enough, change *can* happen. She hopes that the same will happen in reaction to Jonesboro or other nationally publicized crimes by juveniles.

# YOUNG AND ARRESTLESS

1.  Recidivism is the tendency to lapse into a previous pattern of behavior, especially a return to criminal activity. Current juvenile court policies give young criminals a chance for retribution and a clean slate, which makes it hard to determine repeat offenses.

2.  Labeling theory is explained in paragraphs 11 and 12. Students can argue for and against its effectiveness and attempt to explain whether a criminal intentionally labels him/herself by committing a crime.

3.  Strain theory is detailed in paragraph 10. Its connection to current expungment policies is primarily that it seems dependent on the crimes committed and if a criminal stated reasons for acting in such a way. The percentage of those who commit crimes is assumed, under the strain theory, to be those who have been denied societal advancement. Ask students to discuss who is denied these days—always those in minority positions? Denial could be seen as more universal.

4.  Direct students to paragraphs 18 and 20. In sum, expungment interferes with law enforcement because judges will not know of previous offenses and will assign lesser sentences to those they believe to be first-time offenders. Funk argues that society as a whole will suffer expungment practices because judges unknowingly return more career criminals to the streets.

5.  Funk's essay structure is inductive in that its opening example sets up the specific problems with the current juvenile criminal justice system. What follows is his general commentary on the issue, how other sources have addressed the issue, and subsequent recommendations. Ask students to rate its effectiveness with the essays read thus far on the same topic.

# GIVING UP ON THE YOUNG

1. Males and Docuyanan believe adult punishment for juvenile criminals is not an effective means of decreasing recidivism. They feel such severe punishment gives up on these younger human beings and makes things worse for society. For more specific comparisons to Funk, Collier, and Reilly, break students into groups and have them recapitulate each of the four articles to note the particular differences in opinion among them.

2. Paragraph 9 cites rising youth poverty as the reason for the rise in juvenile crime. Alert students will see Males and Docuyanan's ideas evoking the "Strain Theory" of Funk's article. In brief, both essays make a statement that those living in poverty have been denied the institutional means of achieving culturally defined goals; therefore, their reaction is criminal behavior.

3. As preparation for the first exercise under "For Research," have students begin to examine the many paragraphs that include statistical data in the form of ratios and percentages. Arguing against these statistics is an open discussion activity that can begin by evaluating the credibility of the sources from which these statistics come.

4. Paragraphs 26, 27 and 30 all comment on the acceptance gangs provide, as well as the power they offer. Males and Docuyanan feel gangs are not as racially defined as before; instead, they are made up of economically defensive youths.

5. This paragraph suggests gangs are a public-health problem, which could be understood as stemming from a lack of familial involvement or parental supervision. Discuss the fact that it is "the low social, educational, and economic status of the families and communities [that] violent youths come from." Building off the answers to question 1, ask students to rate the effectiveness of this argument in comparison

to the others in this casebook to see if it changes their perspective on the issue of juvenile crime.

## CRUEL PUNISHMENT FOR JUVENILES

1. Smith and Chester's example of Frankie supprots their argument against serious punishment for juveniles. His case was probably chosen to attempt to make the audience aware that such cases happen, namely, the extreme punishment of a youth who did not merit such treatment.

2. Open to discussion, but from the way Frankie is described in the opening paragraphs, the crime he committed, his physical appearance, and the language the authors mark him using, "wow" and "gee," students will likely agree that there was little need for Frankie to "learn a lesson." In fact, students may question the likelihood that Frankie represents a real person–it sounds more like Beaver Cleaver was locked up here. It seems unlikely that Frankie's parents would wish to teach their son a lesson if he were truly a first time offender. There may be more to Frankie's record than Smith and Chester reveal in their essay.

3. Student answers will vary.

4. Paragraphs 10-12 argue legislation embraces punishment over prevention. The authors feel if guns were banned, then gun-related offenses would decrease. They explicitly state, "the increased rate of homicides by juveniles nationally is largely due to the proliferation of guns in this country, not the changed nature of children."

5. Their use of "we know" sets up an authoritative tone. Students are given the biographical information in the headnote that states Smith and Chester are affiliated with the Criminal Justice Institute at Harvard University, from which they may assume the "we" is a legal and criminal justice-learned group. Ask them to compare this information

with the headnotes of some of the other authors read thus far. Does it make their argument more valid or are they in disagreement with fellow criminal justice/legal scholars? Would our perception of them as authorities change if we did not know this biographical data?

6. Paragraph 17 suggests television helps promote this racist point of view regarding juvenile offenders. Ask students to watch their local news or read a local newspaper for a week to see what races are predominantly reported committing serious crimes.

TOUGH JUSTICE FOR JUVENILES

1. Humes is directly quoting Reilly who also used this same word to refer to juvenile offenders  By putting the word in quotation marks, he makes the word Reilly's term. He is, in effect, throwing the word back at him. He uses this word in his argument because the problems with the current system lie in how the legal profession views young offenders.   The word "predator" is presumably much easier to prosecute than the word "child." Humes' argument is that juvenile courts return to their original mission—dealing with young people before they become hardened criminals.

2. The examples of Ronald and George demonstrate the serious problems with the current system. He tells us more of George, perhaps because he spent his life in the system and to emphasize that it was its structure that caused his time in jail more than his behaviors. Moreover, Ronald's story is far more disturbing and could actually work counter to Humes' argument, for Ronald was a juvenile offender as well.

3. Knowing that it costs $25,000 to imprison a felon supports Humes' view that we not give all juvenile criminals adult sentences, especially those like George whose actions did not merit such a severe sentence.

4. Humes tells the story of a frustrated system. Courts become harried with the amount of cases to handle so those inexperienced prosecutors

begin to not pay as close attention to the details that should matter when deciding to treat children as adults. They overlook the mission of preventing recidivism.

5. Student answers will vary.

PEACE IN THE STREETS

1. According to Canada, America values the wrong role models as heroes. The lack of heroes results in children not having any hope for the future. Students can discuss whether they feel children need people to fight for them. The class may discuss who is viewed as heroes among urban youth and if this choice of heroes harms them in any way.

2. Ask for student opinions to this question. His tone could be taken as direct and factual, or as naïve, misguided or even pompous.

3. Canada's personal experience introduces the problem that many American children are living in a world where they need more protection and guidance than ever before. Readers can admire his attempts to reach out to a community and help to give these children a role model. Whether these actions make him more credible can be debated, especially considering his playing the role of hero by resorting to "cheap tricks and theatrics."

4. Assign student groups to evaluate his solutions separately then have them discuss his overarching goals to rate their feasibility.

5. The implied inside enemy is the current state of affairs in our media, family structures, lack of gun legislation, and replacement of neighborhood heroes with drug dealers.
6. Canada offers statistical percentages and personal observations. Whether students find the conclusions based on this evidence logical is open to discussion. One point of contention they could address is that

although Canada states, "Violence is not just a problem of the inner cities or of the minorities in this country," his concluding paragraph includes a racially slanted question: "What happens when those American children are mostly black and brown?" Do students consider the blanket comments he makes about the universal problem of violence consistent with the rest of his article that bases itself on the situations minorities face?

# CHAPTER SIXTEEN
## CASEBOOK: TEEN PARENTS – CHILDREN HAVING CHILDREN?

### TEENAGE PREGNANCY: A PREVENTABLE CALAMITY

1. Sylvester's opening paragraphs list some of the negative consequences of teenage pregnancy such as poverty and the fatherless/dysfunctional family cycle it creates. Have students discuss these issues and add their own.

2. Student answers will vary but make sure they all have an understanding of the term "complacent." Is America a complacent country in which to be a teenage parent as proven by the statistics Sylvester gives?

3. Ask students to define this term as a class. Considering both parts of the term separately, "moral" and "relativism," used together, it seems to suggest a comparison of or perhaps a decision between good and bad, although how one is to gauge between the two is undefined. Teenage pregnancy is a situation which Sylvester feels can no longer be reduced to moral relativism because its consequences are long lasting and cyclical.

4. Students may find themselves referring to early American history to answer this question about "common values." They may be surprised to learn that almost 40% of all babies born in colonial America were conceived out of wedlock. However, the value system of that time mandated that couples marry. "Common values" often refer to a media fabricated definition of the nuclear family unit of the 1950's. However, as social scientists will verify, we are trying to uphold an image that really never existed except on television. Ask students to voice what they think common values are, and from where this value system comes.

5. First ask students who they feel the "we" is that Sylvester speaks as/for. After considering this, have students debate for and against "insisting" to determine why she sees it as a solution. Could it intensify the problem?

6. Break students up into four groups to each represent one of Sylvester's solutions. Have them collaborate to address the feasibility, i.e., pros and cons of each. Then have the four groups converse with one another to state an *overall* understanding as to what Sylvester is advocating.

## CONSTRUCTING AN EPIDEMIC

1. Luker claims the Eisenhower presidency marks the time period of the real teen pregnancy "epidemic." With its "poodle skirts," though, the time period sounds more uniform and innocent compared to the current chaotic world we live in and the current teen pregnancy situation. Since Eisenhower's time, there has been a contraception revolution, the legalization of abortion, an increase in the number of divorces and subsequent restructuring of family units. Students could draw up a time line of social reactions to the problem of teen pregnancy since Luker offers many dates and commentary on their effects.

2. Paragraph 3 attributes the skewed perspective of the problem to the pregnancy rate being determined by a combination of the abortion rate and birth rate. She explains that people assumed the rise in pregnancy was entirely due to the rise in abortions and concerned themselves with the problem of pregnancy rather than abortion.

3. Luker claims teens are over-represented in statistics. Paragraphs 7-10 discuss the misrepresented profile and then explain why this was inaccurate. Ask students to return to the "As You Read" suggestion and talk about whether they are more likely to accept Luker's version

of the problem more than others read in this section of readings because of her explanations.

4. In thinking about the term "epidemic," ask students to bring in clippings from newspapers and magazines as well as details from television or movie plots that include a pregnant teen character/storyline. Students can use these examples to illustrate the differences among presentations of the situation and then to determine if it is really an "epidemic" or not.

5. Beginning in paragraph 10, Luker details the reasons why teens are used as scapegoats. By paragraph 13, students will notice that teens are often used as an outlet for various social ills. Since there are many issues mentioned (poverty, racial inequalities, illegitimacy, etc.), discuss these issues in general and then hear their opinions on why they think the blame is placed on teens.

TEENAGE CHILDBEARING AND PERSONAL RESPONSIBILITY: AN ALTERNATIVE VIEW

1. Have students discuss their assumptions as representatives of teen American society. Can they imagine teenage pregnancies as wanted occurrences? Geronimus' assertion can be found in paragraphs 2 and 3. It is likely sociologists and politicians would disagree with him and demand more factual evidence. One may pose the idea that economics and raising children are hardly ever a perfect fit—having a child is a costly endeavor. Why, then, would someone underage consciously want to depend on the government or other family members for money for an indeterminable period of time? Ask student to discuss this idea.

2. Student answers will vary but make sure to hear their opinions on how a parent's life span relates to raising a child.

3. Open for discussion. Ask students to contrast paragraphs 10 and 11. Geronimus' logic does not seem to be consistent from one paragraph

to another. If students note this, ask them which ideas they agree with more than others.

4. Geronimus brings up the idea that the previous authors neglected: some people are never prepared to become parents. But is it appropriate action to have children early in order to learn from that experience? Could this logic be compared to other teen situations? For example, what about alcohol? Some people will never be able to handle liquor, so does that mean they should drink at a young age in order to find out? Discuss this correlation with the class.

5. Student answers will vary. Construct a debate for and against this topic to gauge class feelings about its feasibility.

6. Begin with a discussion of the nuclear family and current alternative formulations of it. How can/do extended family members assist with the children of teens? Is this a solution?

## ADOLESCENT PREGNANCY: WHEN IS IT A PROBLEM, WHAT IS THE SOLUTION?

1. Considering the sensitivity with which America approaches issues these days (the effects of the political correctness movement), such a radical idea as Battin's is not likely to be enforced by those with the political power to do so. Too many would likely dissent. Ask students if they can recall a recent event/proposal that led to a similar amount of controversy as Battin's might and have them discuss the reactions. Ask them how political improbability factored in to the decisions made about their events/proposals to determine whether such improbability is good or bad.

2. Battin's comparison helps to explain what the process of forced teen contraception might be like, but students may find that it generalizes the serious decision of childbearing. Immunization evokes thoughts of fatal diseases. When compared to teen pregnancy this could imply that

pregnancy is merely a negative consequence of sex. Is making a baby the same as catching the measles? Have students discuss their reactions to this comparison.

3. If students find that her logic is inductive, make sure they outline the specific evidence on which she bases her generalization so that they can determine whether it is sound or not.

4. Open to discussion. Direct students to her statement in paragraph 14 about women of "legal adulthood making reproductive choices in a mature way." These seem to be hasty generalizations on Battin's part and students are sure to recognize that her argument may be too neat.

5. As proposed by the suggestion above, who besides Battin says women over 21 are more responsible or could not benefit from such a form of contraception? Battin limits discussion of her measure and also does not address if the control would or could be "re-applied" if the young woman desires.

6. Refer students to paragraph 12 since it brings up the responsibilities required to be a sexually active individual. Besides pregnancy, there is the issue of sexually transmitted diseases. Moreover, teens are in fact more likely to contract a STD than to get pregnant. However, Battin glosses over this side of teen/sex issue. How can one be more important than the other? Ask students to consider why she did not address the implications of both.

## "CHARTER FAMILIES": HOPE FOR THE CHILDREN OF ILLEGITIMACY?

1. As defined in paragraph 9, the AFDC is a program created by Title IV and was added to the Social Security Act of 1935. Have students note the ideas in paragraphs 9-11 before looking at the rest of the essay to determine whether Wilson offers proof that the AFDC has become a way of life for people. For example, is his use of the statistics from the

Department of Health and Human Services consistent with the ideas on the AFDC?

2.  Make sure students all have an understanding of Wilson's term "destigmatized illegitimacy." To answer these questions students might benefit from comparing the term and Wilson's ideas here to the "moral relativism" and "America's common values" described in the Sylvester article.

3.  Beginning in paragraph 19, Wilson offers his recommendations for a charter home plan. Since he explicitly states "all levels of government and the private sector" are needed for his strategy to work, students might not categorize opponents and proponents by political affiliation. Nevertheless, knowing the overarching goals of each political party can lead to discussion of which might support the plan more/less.

4.  Student answers will vary. Debating the ideas of "punishment" and "the end justifying the means" will spark evaluations of Wilson's plan.

5.  Ask students to compare what they have read about teenage pregnancy during high school (if anything at all) with these 5 articles that discuss its alternate viewpoints/solutions. Has their role as an audience changed since high school? Address how the success of Wilson's essay hinges upon his audience agreeing with his platform. It is unlikely that this speech would be successful if addressed to the average high-school assembly.

# CHAPTER SEVENTEEN
## *THE BLACK FREEDOM STRUGGLE: ARGUMENTS THAT SHAPED HISTORY*

## EDUCATION: OPENING THE SCHOOLHOUSE DOORS

### BROWN V. BOARD OF EDUCATION OF TOPEKA (1954)

1. The first paragraph details the various important functions of education as follows: the means to good citizenship; what is required to perform public responsibilities; what awakens children to cultural values needed for professional life; and what is necessary to succeed. Students can discuss if these values are consistent with today's views of what an "educated person" is.

2. The decision regarding law school is applicable to elementary and secondary schooling because these places are where children learn about the "real world" of social interaction. The Supreme Court made this analogy to prove that it is nonsensical to keep races apart from each other in schools when outside of school (whether in neighborhoods or professionally) they *will* eventually meet.

3. Student answers will vary.

4. The Supreme Court is acknowledging that the nation will surely meet some local difficulties in applying this decision, but they argue that such difficulties can and must be overcome due to the greater necessity of overcoming segregation/racism. The obstacle involved with overturning a system completely is that it takes the general population longer to get used to new rules. In 1954, Americans had limited exposure to structures that deviated from the "whitebread" opinions of the status quo perpetuated by the popular media. Thus, the longer to embrace the concept of integrated school systems.

5. "Separate but equal" was supposed to mean the offering of the same education in separate facilities. Ask students what they think school administrators' arguments were for keeping the races separate. What were they trying to avoid? Considering the ideas about the "real world" mentioned before, racially segregated schools could never be equal because they would never promote the social interaction needed to advance knowledge. They are not consistent with a democratic society because there is no interaction of people to consent or dissent on opinions. Non-association was preferred and legislators in 1896 probably thought blacks would never become professionally equal, no matter how much education they received.

## BLACK MONDAY: SEGREGATION OR AMALGAMATION ...AMERICA HAS A CHOICE

1. Black Monday may refer to multiple issues. The term "black" may promote a sense of bleak hopelessness, a dark age. It also refers to the color of the skin of the individuals striving for freedom and equality. Brady connects the term to negative connotations of the word black in order to reflect his opinion of the Supreme Court decision.

2. Ask students if brief, encapsulated descriptions of historical events can ever be accurate. Although, they work to support his argument because these paragraphs limit themselves to describe the passing of legal measures and declarations, most all of which are slanted towards individual freedoms and rights to be legislated by the state and not Congress. Furthermore, his is grossly inaccurate in his relation of historical facts. African Americans did indeed fight in both the Revolutionary and Civil Wars. They were legally prevented from holding public offices in many states, yet Brady holds them accountable for this failure. His skewed telling of the facts may serve to alienate an educated audience who knows better and can see his slanted evidence for what it is–doctored to support his point at any cost.

3. Open to discussion replacing "African American influence" with names of other immigrant groups to alternate the frames of reference and prove the weakness of Brady's claim.

4. Brady's feelings towards the NAACP seem to be nonchalant and demeaning. He gives only a fact-based history of its creation and downplays black accomplishments: "It entered politics." His views can be seen as hypocritical, though, because he sarcastically shuns the NAACP for their use of excellent judgment in selecting their cases, etc. But he did the same with his rendition of history as proven in question 2. Ask students to discuss why/how it is he can be judgmental of their power and use of their intelligence when he uses the same tactics.

5. Begin with a brief discussion of the differences between the powers of the Supreme Court and Congress. What do students know already? The true question Black Monday decided was: Does the Supreme Court the power to establish by a decree a national segregation policy which would bind all of the 48 states—a power which Congress itself does not possess? He feels the Supreme Court's decision has no foundation because it does not possess legislative power. Therefore, it cannot make a decree which could have the effect of an act of Congress. He smugly notes, though, that such "violation of the Constitution" and "invasion of the province of Congress" has happened before.

## THE SOUTHERN MANIFESTO

1. The Southern Manifesto probably employs this phrase to comment on the need of a government document with a foundation that does not allow revisions based on "popular" opinions. However, students will likely agree that the Brown decision was not a reaction to "popular passion" but to a general injustice—racial oppression and unequal treatment.

2. The social and political implications are that 96 *white* politicians representing 11 states wrote this manifesto to state that the South as a whole wanted to resist the Brown decision. Moreover, because it is well documented that most blacks were kept from voting in southern states, these politicians did not represent the black voice of the south. Ask students if they feel that there could also have been a Northern Manifesto. Since the main argument is that there is a national problem with the Brown decision, and national chaos and confusion in school systems, why or why not?

3. Open to discussion. Refer back to the Brown V. Board of Education reading to look for statements that could infer future troubled relations between races.

4. The logic of the Southern Manifesto is based on references to other government institutional practices (system of checks and balances, 14th amendment, etc.) and legal cases (Roberts v. City of Boston, Plessy v. Ferguson, Lum v. Rice), all of which students can evaluate for their relevance to the claim the Southern Manifesto is making. In detailing its strengths and weaknesses, compare the manifesto to the Brown reading. The key message is that we must use the power of public opinion and trust in the system of U.S. government to reverse the Brown decision. Direct students to the "we" closing statements that seem to alternate between Constitutionally-based and socially-based issues. Who is "we?"

DEATH AT AN EARLY AGE

1. This Boston classroom was indeed separate but not at all equal in its educational policies. Discuss the classroom's appearance and what a non-ghetto classroom looks like to discuss its implications further.

2. Open to discussion. Students may be able to bring in examples (textual and media-based) to chronicle the changes in education and society over the past 30 years.

3. The classroom situation is connected to the Brown decision because it is a ghetto classroom. Although we are not told of the exact racial make up, the "separate" idea is still in existence here. The idea of a Hebrew school could also be argued as "separate," but differs in that its curriculum differs (not "equal" or equated to the education system questioned in Brown.)

4. Open to discussion. Ultimate responsibility could be argued to lie in the hands of the U.S. government, state legislatures, school administrators, teachers, parents, etc.

5. Recognizing "collusion" as the secret actions to achieve a fraudulent, illegal or deceitful purpose, Kozol's friend makes a valid point about Kozol's place of employment. The idea of "curriculum deviation" as the reason for Kozol's firing is easy to argue against since students will rebut that the education offered at this school certainly deviated from what should be provided. Kozol's choice of poem being the cause of his firing also makes you wonder why the school suddenly paid attention to his class readings. Perhaps his "speaking out" and "taking [of] forthright action" caused them to probe into his curriculum. Kozol is sent the message from administration that promoting black authors in a predominantly black school will not be (ironically) tolerated.

## NON-VIOLENCE/VIOLENCE: FIGHTING FOR EQUALITY

### LETTER FROM A BIRMINGHAM JAIL

1. Student answers will vary.

2. King's voice is confident and honest. His feelings reflect his argument about nonviolent action as the means to overcome discrimination. He establishes his authority and credibility by stating his credentials within the letter, answering criticisms of his work, and comparing himself and his work to that of St. Paul and Socrates.

3. The status quo in 1963 Birmingham was a white power structure that maintained segregation. Students can discuss their opinions of what the status quo is today. Considering waves of political correctness it seems that while a white power structure is still intact, less discrimination is tolerated.

4. His catalogue of reasons makes vivid the injustices of segregation via images and words.

5. Like question 2, this question asks students to analyze King's voice. Students can partner up and read several paragraphs out loud to each other as if reading a letter. Then one student can present the letter to the rest of the class so to hear any signs of a preaching tone.

6. The sections are indeed effective because he begins with definitions of just and unjust laws. He appeals to authorities (St. Thomas Aquinas, Martin Buber, Paul Tillich, and the 1954 decision of the Supreme Court), then offers examples.

THE PROVOCATION OF VIOLENCE

1. Howard believes violence can arouse the public at large. Students can discuss if they feel violence can change the opposition's point of view; however, the examples given prove that whether or not a point of view was changed, legislation passed which at least enforces tolerance in some way. To illustrate, the 600 Negroes tear-gassed at Selma, Alabama gave way to the voting bill; the Birmingham bombing caused President Kennedy to pass the Civil Rights bill.

2. Open to discussion. Students can analyze the paragraphs that offer explanations of the types of nonviolent tactics taken as a means to provoke non-violence. Howard asks many questions throughout the piece and students can attempt answers in order to gain a greater understanding of when the line blurs. For instance, "Does a movement which is dedicated to nonviolence as the means of action and reaction

inherently need violence to sustain it?" and when reflecting on the parade captain words, "Did he really mean 'no lives'? Or was he refusing to admit even to himself that the nonviolent movement often thrives on violence?"

3. The feeling of shame resulted from not getting through to the courthouse—physically by violence or non-violence, or civically to change the laws regarding discrimination. Their voices were not heard; they did not change any minds that day. The question also arises, did they feel a sense of failure not only because they did not get into the court house, but because they had failed to incite the police into violent action against the demonstration?

4. Howard's argument is structured on the question and answer she sets up: When is the provocation of violence more than a calculated risk of the movement? When the movement adopts a goal which it believes can be fulfilled only through violence, then this list of reasons as to why we are drawn to violence support her argument as they prove violence has power to arouse the public at large. This may be a stand students have not considered before—that the success of a non-violent protest actually depends on inciting a violent reaction in authorities— ask their opinions on whether her reasoning is logical.

5. The provocation of violence can be interpreted and misinterpreted in many ways. It is a subjective concept. Even Howard admits, "The impact on the public at large depends on the character of the victim." In effect, if the victim is not "noticeable," the violence can backfire. If the victim looks innocent and helpless, moral outrage will be bestowed on the attackers. They key is to look like a peaceful demonstration was outright attacked by unyielding aggressors.

6. Howard's tone seems objective, although at times it is hard to figure out if she is for or against the actions she describes. However, she does acknowledge that the provocation of violence works.

# MESSAGE TO THE GRASS ROOTS

1. The common enemy is identified as the white man. He notes that some blacks feel some whites are not enemies, "but time will tell." He hopes to achieve unity among blacks so to go about solving the problems of oppression, exploitation, and discrimination. Later in his speech, Malcolm X states, "We need to stop airing our differences in front of the white man, put the white man out of our meetings, and then sit down and talk shop with each other."

2. He defines the black race this way so to call them together. He recognizes the diversity within his own race, but then ironically classifies all whites as blond and blue-eyed. He denies whites the same individuality, although his argument is based on unification. Students may feel that this classifying is logical since X wants all blacks to come together to fight the white oppression.

3. X's citing of revolutions is to stress the unification it takes to mount a revolution: "When you study the historic nature of revolutions, the motives of revolutions, the objectives of revolutions, the results of revolutions, and the methods used in a revolution, you may change your words." This promotion of a black revolution differs from Martin Luther King's message of non-violence; revolutions cause bloodshed.

4. African Americans who work within the established social system are termed house slaves and modern Uncle Toms. They are then compared to novocain since they teach the masses of field slaves to suffer peacefully. Audience is important to the success of this article because he is attempting to persuade members of the same race and religious conviction to come together and retaliate against discrimination. Problematic is that he has not considered those who may have never felt the harsh discrimination he describes and dismisses those who do not consider all whites the common enemy.

5. Malcolm X might be impatient with Jan Howard's ideas of violence as a provocation of risk. His argument is based on starting a revolution,

which implies a direct tactic of violence. Students can outline each author's intentions of using violence and compare.

## EQUAL OPPORTUNITY: OUTLAWING DISCRIMINATION

MY DUNGEON SHOOK

1. Baldwin says that whites do not expect African Americans to aspire to excellence. They are expected to make peace with mediocrity. "Society" here refers to the white race. As Baldwin expresses to his nephew, "You have been told [by society] where you could go and what you could do (and how you could do it) and where to live and whom you could marry."

2. African Americans who trust their experience and know from whence they came are presented as morally and intellectually superior. Whites are not as superior because they are "innocent people who are trapped in a history they do not understand." They are trapped by this history in that they have been told for years that "black men are inferior to white men." Baldwin admits that some whites know better than this but find it difficult to act on what they know, which sustains the entrapment.

3. In the line previous to this quote Baldwin tells his nephew of whites "who believed that your [black] imprisonment made them safe [now] are losing their grasp of reality." Thus, these "brothers" include whites who must see and face that the white status quo is not the true (or deserving) reality.

4. Baldwin may have chosen this date because it is the centennial of black "freedom." Even after 100 years, there is still a need for blacks to fight the white status quo. He also chronicles the minor changes in feelings of whites and blacks over the years.

5.  Baldwin's title refers to lines by a great poet who he classifies with other dignified black men. The message of the poem and the title of his essay seems to be for the next generation to continue to fight for equality.

PRESIDENT'S SPEECH: JUNE 11, 1963

1.  This is a moral issue rather than a legal or political one because laws and partisanship have little to do with the individual morality between Americans. Kennedy cites both Scripture and the Constitution because both are codes of morality. The Scriptural reference he implies is "Do unto others and you would have them do unto you." This supports Kennedy's view for equal rights and opportunities for Americans.

2.  The "promise" is the freedom supposedly granted to blacks in Lincoln's Emancipation Proclamation in 1863. Kennedy recognizes that the heirs to these slaves are not yet truly free. They are "not yet freed from the burden of injustice; they are not yet freed from social and economic oppression." The fulfillment of this promise is to be achieved through legislation and on an individual basis.

3.  Open to discussion.

4.  Kennedy's speech is directed to all of the American public; however, it seems to be informing whites who have yet to realize the moral dilemma of the changes that need to be made and will be made. Black audience members are specifically referred to as Kennedy acknowledges their courage but also remarks that the moral crisis cannot be solved by demonstrations in the streets. It is especially important that Kennedy consider his audience because it was a political reaction to the preceding events of racial discrimination. This speech also promises to enact legislation that will effect every American community so he would have had to consider the best way to present it.

5. Student answers will vary.

## FROM SHARECROPPER TO LOBBYIST

1. The tone of Hamer's essay is a mixture of control and triumph. Her message is likely to be readily accepted because it does not outright blame whites or complain of unfair treatment. It simply states the facts of her story and the treatment she was subjected to.

2. The details Hamer offers of her and her parents' lives on the plantation as sharecroppers offer insight into the condition of poverty employed to keep African Americans politically impotent. The other tactics Hamer describes are barring blacks from voting and preventing them from attending precinct meetings. Hamer feels this strategy by the whites is hypocritical because they are breaking laws that they set up.

3. Hamer is trying to reach fellow blacks in this essay. She wants to establish the black power to vote and a united fight for the things they deserve as Americans. Students can openly discuss their opinions on the effectiveness of the essay. They will likely note the lack of flow in the opening paragraphs as distracting, but Hamer's account of her life in the political arena is more direct.

4. Hamer tells those whites that she can and will stay in America because it is her right to do so. In Africa, Hamer is treated better and she sees blacks with all of the positions of authority held by whites in America. A discussion of North versus South can ensue in response to whether or not Hamer's experience would have been different in Detroit or Boston. The South was different in Hamer's time because of the sharecropping plantations, but do students feel the South is still racially intolerant and a place to exploit the condition of poverty?

## THE BEGINNINGS OF A NEW AGE

1. The "new Negro" could be all blacks following the principles demonstrated by Rosa Parks. A "new Negro" is one that sees him/herself as an important contributor to the economic, social, political, and spiritual progress of a great nation. The "white city fathers" were concerned about these emerging people because they had not encountered such a united and strong (50,000 people in total) retaliation to the white status quo.

2. The "white people" described here is everyone white in Montgomery who felt threatened by blacks demonstrating any power over the city. This includes whites with legal authority and those without. There are many examples students can find of whites trying to thwart black efforts for justice but some include ticketing black-owned vehicles, harassing blacks on the telephone, and attacking them on the street.

3. The arrest of Rosa Parks caused black citizens to realize they were not "defenseless against the unlawful cruelties of their oppressors." The boycott increased their determination and resolve to the level of Patrick Henry: "Give me liberty or give me death."

4. Students can locate various examples of black unification but one mentioned is the formation of carpools. This unity subsequently restored dignity because the black population realized their power and worth in the economic life of the city.

5. Student answers will vary.

# REFLECTIONS ON THE STRUGGLE: LOOKING BACK, MOVING FORWARD

## THE NEXT RECONSTRUCTION

1. The segregation in Atlanta today is voluntary—often indistinguishable, but still color-coded. Although peaceful, this system is not conducive to racial harmony. It is peaceful coexistence—a wary truce between two groups who believe they are fundamentally different and will always live separately.

2. Jacoby's feelings about Malcolm X are summarized in the following statement: "In the name of peace, well-meaning liberals encouraged the Black Power movement, even glamorized it, rather than committing the nation to the hard work of addressing the discontent that gave rise to black demagogues." The drawbacks of cultural identity are no real political power, equality, or respect between the races.

3. Social inequality refers to economics and poverty. It posed a greater challenge because there were no shortcut answers to the frustration that drove black youths to violence. Tension between the races can build up, but the economic strife that occurs *within* neighborhoods as a result of white dominance is more difficult to monitor. Blacks confronted this new enemy through riots, looting and burning down their own broken-down communities.

4. Student answers will vary.

## MAYBE SEGREGATION WASN'T SO DAMAGING

1. The common assumption is that integrated is essentially better. Kane thinks the NAACP may be wrong because some black students, as he did, received fine educations in segregated schools and were not

harmed by non-intermingling of the races. Students can discuss whether this education was the norm for black schools.

2. Mordecai Gist Elementary School was the only school of Kane's that was integrated. It is evident in his discussion of Harlem Park Junior High School that Kane feels positively about his education in segregated schools; however, he is not as straightforward in his description of his elementary school years. Ask students to analyze his comment, "The teachers at the inherently inferior segregated schools of West Baltimore educated me as best they could." He uses sarcasm to point out that these teachers were at least equal to those in integrated schools, even if the outside world did not think they were.

3. Mr. Golden taught Kane about the "real world." In addition to Black history, Mr. Golden informed his students of the history happening at that time—the "Civil Rights movement and all the protagonists and antagonists therein." He also set up his classroom for competition, another aspect of future academic and professional environments. Discussion can ensue from speculation of curriculums in the less segregated schools at that time.

4. Open to discussion.

5. and 6. The overall tone of this piece is one of pride. Kane is proud to have been educated in a segregated school system. His tone when employing the words of the Supreme Court decision of Brown v. Board of Education is sarcastic at times. He repeatedly uses the phrase "inherently unequal" to challenge the Brown decision's logic and to support his point that the segregated schools he attended were not such.

WHITES SAY I MUST BE ON EASY STREET

1. The "stigma" of affirmative action Painter's student describes is that others believe that she was accepted into Harvard because she was

black and not because she was qualified. This stigma touches both students and professors in the academic world. While it is unlikely that minority students can avoid the stigma, they can overcome it by proving themselves and overachieving to gain recognition.

2. Painter approves of affirmative action policies; however, she wants opponents to realize that "they are reciting the same old white superiority line." Her admission of the negative aspects of affirmative action does not detract from her argument because, as students will likely agree, these are already unstated and/or stated assumptions.

3. Student answers will vary.

4. "Being helped" infers that one is not fully qualified. For instance, ask students if they think Painter would have been hired without affirmative action, and only on her Harvard degree, the quality of her dissertation, and hard work. The class can argue yes or no based on the feelings of being helped and being "qualified."

5. If affirmative action were dismantled, the result would be, says Painter, the "same old discrimination—unneedful of new clothes": "whites are better than blacks; men are better than women." Students can openly discuss whether they think affirmative action could and would be dismantled if no one admits it is helping.

## GHETTOIZED BY BLACK UNITY

1. The prevailing identity is a concept of "blackness" grounded in the spirit of black power. Out of Malcolm X's movement, "it carried a righteous anger at and mistrust of American society…" Whether or not a movement can define an identity of an entire race is open to discussion.

2. A collective identity can be invasive and hinder you from experiencing the opportunity America has to offer, according to Steele. If you are

defined by your fight for your ethnic identity, you do not take the time to form your own. Steele offers the example of his own struggle to argue against such identities. Steele feels that blacks are shamed by their own race into embracing an identity and culture that they may not wish to. Moreover, any dissent from this identity is viewed as "selling out to whites" and denying one's cultural identity and history. Steele feels that when you suspend the racial-identity struggle and live as an individual in America, you discover the opportunity it offers. Students can debate whether or not such pride can prevent progress.

3. Steele thinks it is easier to remain resentful because it prevents accountability. As long as resentment and anger define the black experience, blacks will not be held accountable for failure. The blame is always displaced. Steele feels that it is this fear of failure that prevents many blacks from taking chances and grabbing the opportunities available to them. Their resentment keeps them oppressed.

4. Students can research Martin Luther King's writings to determine what he said about the "promised land." Based on the writing of King's in this chapter, students will likely define his "promised land" as a racially tolerant America that did not become that way through violence. Steele's "promised land" is an America where blacks realize their opportunity.